BREMEN
EUROPA

INCRES LINE
The Friendly Way

No. 8   APRIL 1951

S.S. EUROPA

NEW YORK — PLYMOUTH —
AND HAVRE

PASSENGER
FARE AND

SAILING SCHEDULE
TO EUROPE

General Passenger Agents
ARNOLD BERNSTEIN SHIPPING COMPANY, Inc.
17 BATTERY PLACE   NEW YORK 4, N. Y.
HAnover 2-7400

NORWEGIAN AMERICA
LINE

DIRECT SAILINGS
TO & FROM
NORWAY

M.S. "BATORY"

Direct to
SOUTHAMPTON · COPENHAGEN
GDYNIA

GDYNIA AMERICA LINE

1951 SAILING LIST

SAILING SCHEDULE AND MINIMUM PASSAGE RATES
DIRECT TO NORTHERN EUROPE

Between
NEW YORK
and
GOTHENBURG
Sweden

SWEDISH AMERICAN LINE

SHORT ROUTE TO
NORTHERN EUROPE

NEW REVISED RATES

AMERICAN EXPRESS CO.
Travel Department
65 Broadway
New York, N. Y.

NO. 18, MAY 25, 1951   CANCELLING ALL PREVIOUS ISSUES

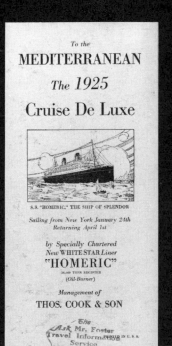

To the
MEDITERRANEAN
The 1925
Cruise De Luxe

S.S. "HOMERIC," THE SHIP OF SPLENDOR

*Sailing from New York January 24th
Returning April 1st*

*by Specially Chartered
New WHITE STAR Liner*
"HOMERIC"
34,500 TONS REGISTER
(Oil-Burner)

Management of
THOS. COOK & SON

The
Ask Mr. Foster
Travel Information
Service
L. S. DONALDSON CO.
MINNEAPOLIS

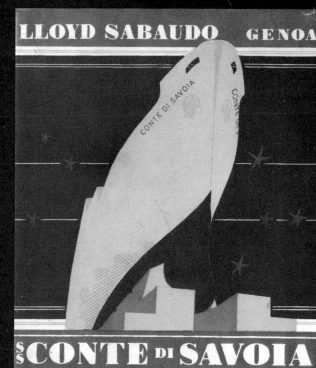

LLOYD SABAUDO   GENOA

CONTE DI SAVOIA

SS CONTE DI SAVOIA

FIFTY FAMOUS LINERS

Frank O. Braynard FRS & William H. Miller

W.W. Norton and Company

NEW YORK   LONDON

The brilliant launching of the France in May 1960, witnessed by thousands including President and Madame de Gaulle.

First American Edition 1982

ISBN 0-393-01611-0

This book is dedicated to
JAMES G CROSSON
who has overcome enormous adversity so as to help others

Front cover photograph by Ernest Arroyo

Photoset in 10 on 11 pt Garamond
by Manuset Ltd, Baldock, Herts.
Printed in Great Britain on 115 gsm Fineblade
coated cartridge,
and bound, by The Garden City Press, Letchworth, Herts

Contents

Introduction I

Ships are the largest moving objects made by man. Ocean liners are to many the most appealing of all ships. My passion to draw liner sketches, write books about ships, and otherwise spread the fun has been lifelong. I can vividly remember my joy at getting a supply of 'shirt cardboards' (pieces of grey cardboard used to give freshly laundered and ironed shirts a nice body) as they were ideal for drawing ship pictures. This was when I was six years old. A drawing I made of the *Leviathan* when I was seven (1923) is used in the jacket flap of my series on that great liner. I have always been very happy to find others who are equally interested in passenger ships. This book is very much a labour of love because it is such great fun to share my love of liners.

Bill Miller, my co-author, has an equal passion for ocean liners and it is a treat to work with him on this book. He has written 38 of the 50 chapters, while I contributed the other 12 and the 50 pen sketches and most of the photographs used. We have enjoyed the assignment tremendously. The only real problem was selecting the ships. Hundreds of other ocean liners, large and small, had a perfect right to be in this book, and we know it very well. But we have made a stab at it and only hope, most sincerely, that we will be asked by Patrick Stephens to produce another book that could well be entitled *Fifty Famous Liners II*. We encourage our readers to write in with suggested names of ships they would like us to include in our projected second volume. Who can tell, we may even need a third!

Frank O Braynard
Sea Cliff, New York

Introduction II

The great ocean liners parallel characters in a long-running drama. They are members of an immortal cast, one that remains both exciting and alluring.

There is the sense of triumph among them—such as with the brilliantly successful career of the first *Mauretania* and still later with the *Queen Mary*. Others had exceptionally long and useful lives—such as the *Virginian* of 1905, which lasted 50 years, and the former *Albert Ballin*, which is now nearing 60. Others had incalculable impact, both on their times and on history, such as the tragedy of the *Lusitania* or the brief appearance of the exquisite *Normandie*. Of course, still others come to mind: the undying brisk interest in the *Titanic* and her sinking, the superb success of the *Aquitania*, the revolutionary impact of the *Ile de France*, the horrific loss of life with the demise of the *Cap Arcona*, the genius of the *United States*. Comments could go on for pages.

I visualise considerable debate among the readers of this book on the ships that Frank Braynard and I have selected. Hopefully, a subsequent volume (or volumes) will contain other magical names: *Kaiser Wilhelm der Grosse, Bergensfjord* (1913), *Paris, Vulcania, Empress of Japan, Manhattan*, the second *Mauretania*, and so many others. Much more is yet to be written, more unusual photographs to be shared.

My fascination with these great ships stems from a most happy youth along the shore of Hoboken, New Jersey, just across from the famed liner berths of New York City. Studying and collecting materials of these 'queens' has been a 'second life'. However, an unquestionable highlight has been to share this project (and fortunately several others) with Frank Braynard, a dean among maritime historians and a totally joyous soul. Together, we have poured over his legendary collection: selecting photos, gathering information, examining colourful brochures, watching the project come to life. What enormous fun!

William H Miller
Jersey City, New Jersey

The Mauretania *passing the lower Manhattan skyline, with the stately* Aquitania *inbound. The year, 1932.*

FIFTY
FAMOUS LINERS

Britannia.

Britannia

The Cunard Line was founded by Samuel Cunard and two partners in 1839. It was created to operate a steamship service between Liverpool, Halifax, and Boston, although all its early steamers used sails as well as steam. The company quickly became known as the Cunard Line. Its first steamer was the *Unicorn*, bought from the Burns Line, a coastal packet firm, but its first vessel built especially for transatlantic service was the *Britannia*, and her fame as one of the Atlantic's most famous steamships has long been recognised. She looked much like a sailing ship, with the traditional three masts and square yards, the clipper bow and gilded stern, but there were important differences. She had large, sturdy paddle-wheels, with a walk and railings over the upper half circle of her twin paddle-wheel boxes. The walk was continued both fore and aft from port to starboard, the beginnings of the bridge structure so common to later liners. And she had a relatively thick, straight-up-and-down smokestack. It was painted a special shade of red and had a band of black at the top. Two thin black bands, nothing more than stripes, ringed the stack dividing the red part into three bands, equal in width to the top band of black. The red hue included a strong touch of orange and came to be known as 'Cunard red'.

The *Britannia*'s engines were built on the Clyde by Messrs R Napier and Co. They occupied 70 feet within the 207-foot hull and boasted 420 horsepower. She burned 38 tons of coal a day and could make 8½ knots. Capt Henry Woodruff was in command on July 4 1840 when she set sail from Liverpool on her maiden voyage. Among the 63 passengers on this historic trip was Samuel Cunard. The crossing took 12 days and 10 hours to Halifax. After a brief stop she went on to Boston.

Only cabin passengers were carried on the fast mail ships of this day, with emigrants continuing to crowd aboard sailing craft. The new *Britannia* carried fuel, cargo, crew, and passengers on four decks. Coal occupied most of the lower area, with a cargo hold far forward. Two more cargo holds bracketed the long engine space on the next level, with a sail locker at the stem and a wine cellar far aft. Rooms for mail and specie were forward, with stores aft. A small living space amidships aft took care of the stewards. The third level contained passenger cabins that could accommodate 115 persons. Compared with more modern vessels the spaces were minimal, but in 1840 they were luxurious. The tiny 'ladies cabin', amidships and just aft of the engine, was made famous by being depicted on an elegant issue of lavender-coloured chinaware known as the 'Boston Mail'. Tufted sofas, handsome chandeliers, and decorative wooden panelling gave a sense of elegance and comfort. In addition to private staterooms for passengers, both aft and forward, there was the traditional 'glory hole' for seamen at the prow, a space for firemen, and cabins for the two top engineering officers. Two circular staircases aft linked the cabins with the main saloon aft on the upper deck. The Captain and his Chief Officer had private cabins on the starboard and port sides of the area farthest aft on this deck, the wheelhouse being between them. The main saloon, also shown on various pieces of the 'Boston Mail' china, was large enough to fit two long dining tables. Couches on the outer sides and two long, fixed benches on the inner sides allowed passengers to sit at these tables.

Forward of this one large public room was a pantry, a hatch, and a skylight over the engine space. Forward of the stack was the galley, more skylights, and the officers' mess. Small cabins for stewards, the purser, a baker, cooks, a carpenter, and boatswains were located around the stack and on the inner face of the paddle boxes. There was a 'cow house' next to the butcher's cabin which provided fresh milk.

The career of this sturdy pioneer Atlantic steamer was not a long one under the golden lion houseflag of Cunard. After 40 round trips she was sold to the Germans and renamed *Barbarosa*. Her machinery was removed and she became a sailing ship in the Prussian Navy. In 1880 she was sunk while being used as a target ship—a sad ending for any liner.

Gross tonnage: 1,154
Length overall: 207 feet
Width: 34 feet
Machinery: Two-cylinder, side-lever steam
Speed: 8½ knots
Capacity: 115 passengers
Built: Robert Duncan, Greenock, Scotland
Demise: Sunk 1880 as target ship

Left *A model of the* Britannia *made by August F Crabtree in The Mariners Museum, Newport News, Virginia* (Courtesy of The Mariners Museum, Newport News).

Right *A piece of fine china made for the* Britannia (Courtesy of Charles Sachs).

Left *A model of the* Britannia *afloat in the pool of the greatest Cunarder* Queen Elizabeth.

Right *A stateroom on the* Britannia, *the one used in 1842 by Charles Dickens.*

Left *The* Britannia *leaving Boston through the ice, an engraving later banned by the Massachusetts port as bad publicity.*

Washington

America entered the transatlantic steamship scene in 1847. The first ship to fly the 'Stars and Stripes' in regular transoceanic service on the Atlantic was the *Washington.* It may also be said that she was the beginning of the North German Lloyd, for she was built not only with a US government subsidy but with financial aid from merchants of Bremen.

The *Washington* was launched January 31 1847, at the yard of Westervelt and Mackay, New York. She was said to be the world's largest steamship at the time. With much the same silhouette as other early Atlantic liners, she had three masts, large wooden paddle boxes, a bowsprit and sailing ship bow, and squared off stern. Those who cheered as she slid down the ways called her 'the most complete and beautiful ever constructed'. It was proudly predicted that she would prove to be the fastest steamship in the world. Her black hull had a white band painted around it with imitation gunports, as many sailing ships had. This was originally a device to scare off pirates in the Far East, but had come to be a traditional style of painting in large vessels. A full-length figurehead of George Washington was at the prow.

The maiden voyage of the Oceanic Steam Navigation Company's *Washington* was not all that her owners might have wanted. Cunard's *Britannia* sailed from Boston on the same day and beat her

across by more than two full days. At Southampton the welcome was dampened by unfriendly press accounts. A reporter for *The Times*, of London, called her 'about as ugly a specimen of steamship building as ever went through this anchorage'. Another writer said that 'she seemed to roll along rather than steam through the water'.

The liner's arrival at Bremerhaven, however, was entirely different. She was the first ocean steamer ever to come up the River Weser, for one thing. On another count, Burgomaster Smidt's son was aboard her, returning home from Louisville, Kentucky. The Burgomaster had his personal pennant flying from the main mast of one of the welcoming ships. The harbour was crowded for the occasion and a goodly fleet of small boats had gone some ways down the Weser to escort the *Washington* up to her berth. Many hundreds watched and cheered as the procession passed. At least two fine oil painters were on hand making quick sketches and notes from which to create paintings of the ship and her arrival. Both showed their enthusiasm by putting altogether too many stripes and stars in the huge flag the *Washington* flew. She flew a flag with a most unusual star arrangement, one that was used for only a very short time. Some stars formed four long lines which crossed at the centre of the blue field. Other stars were in a circle centred in the field. Both paintings

have survived and have been widely circulated in print form since that gala day on the Weser.

An enthusiastic formal dinner was offered the *Washington*'s officers and those VIP passengers who had come over on her. There were many speeches linking America and Germany in flowery language. One of the serenading orchestra's members was inspired to compose a 'Washington Polka' on the spot. A six-foot model of the ship was presented to port officials. It was bravely announced that a sister ship would be named *Hermann* in honour of the ancient warrior who had freed the Germans from domination by Rome.

The arrival of the *Washington* on the scene illustrated how important competition was to become in what was rapidly becoming the world's premier passenger-ship service. For instance, she carried two classes of passengers, and she charged only $120 for eastbound passage and $150 westbound, compared to Cunard's $190 for passage either way. Her owners, who came to be known as the Bremen Line, also reduced freight rate charges. But most important, her arrival convinced Cunard that it would have to shift its North American terminal from Boston to New York.

The *Washington* proved to be underpowered and frequent improvements in her boilers had to be made at first. But the service became more regular and her passenger capacity was increased. She had a relatively quiet life except for the one occasion when her master became demented and tried to steer her onto the rocks. The Germans who had aided her financially decided to put their money into a new steamship line of their own and, at about the same time, the US subsidy was not renewed. The ship was laid up in 1857 and sold the next year to Pacific interests. She served briefly on the Panama route, both on the Atlantic and the Pacific sides, and then was laid up as out of date. Steamship design was advancing so rapidly that a 16-year-old ship was considered ancient. In 1864 she was scrapped in San Francisco.

Gross tonnage: 1,640
Length overall: 230 feet
Width: 38 feet
Machinery: Twin side-lever steam engines
Speed: 8 knots
Capacity: 300 passengers
Built: Westervelt & Mackay, New York, 1847
Demise: Scrapped at San Francisco in 1864

The paddler at sea, a reproduction from an oil painting of the Washington.

Above *The* Washington, *headed into the wind, about to rescue all 477 souls aboard the dismasted* Winchester. *From a Currier and Ives print.*

Below *In 1958, co-author Braynard found this 1847 painting of the* Washington. *It was photographed with him by the* New York Times.

Fifty Famous Liners

Great Eastern

There have been many famous Atlantic liners, several before the *Great Eastern* and many after her, but none before or since can quite stand 'as tall' (to borrow an American cowboy phrase) as the extraordinary vessel that was first announced in 1852. She was the brain child of Isambard Kingdom Brunel, tunnel and bridge-builder extraordinaire and already famous for two earlier vessels. There had been his *Great Western*, the first newly-built transatlantic liner to be successful on the run, and his *Great Britain*, the first ocean liner built of iron. Brunel worked with shipbuilder John Scott Russell on his newest monster creation. They named her *Leviathan.* They would run her to India and China, and she would be large enough to carry fuel for the round trip. Even before her keel was laid the ship was unlucky. A rival company got the mail subsidy and the route had to be changed.

The story of this historic ship has often been told. For those who would enjoy a masterwork on the subject, we recommend James Dugan's *The Great Iron Ship.* This was one of the favourite works of William Francis Gibbs, the noted American designer. Whenever he saw important people off aboard the *United States*, his finest achievement, he would present them with a copy. Brunel and Gibbs had much in common.

Virtually everything about the *Leviathan* was of new design. No other ship had ever leaped so far ahead in the evolutionary road of marine architecture and engineering. She had six masts and five stacks; she had sails, a huge propeller, and gigantic paddlewheels; she had a double bottom extending above her waterline and 16 watertight compartments, making her safer than most ships before or after. Her tonnage was nearly six times that of the world's largest ship of that day and she was twice as long. Had she been used on the run intended she might well have proved profitable.

An endless series of misfortunes dogged her. At her launching she crushed several spectators and became stuck on the ways. Her original owners lost faith and bowed out. Brunel drew up a remarkable set of three-dimensional-looking plans, coloured them, and folded them into what looked like a carpet bag. He needed to raise money to complete the ship. One of these plans, bag and all, is owned by Walter Lord, author of the well-known book *A Night To Remember.* More money was subscribed, a new company was formed, and the ship's name was changed to *Great Eastern.* It was decided to run her across the Atlantic, but funds were not adequate to complete her passenger accommodation. She started out for her trials in 1859 only to be the victim of an

explosion killing a number of her crew. Although she was inspected by Queen Victoria and Prince Albert and survived a bad storm at this point, the legend of bad luck continued to grow.

Brunel died before his dream ship began her maiden voyage. Aged only 53, he was struck down by Bright's disease, although many believed it was the five years of hectic effort and disappointments that killed him. On one of *Great Eastern*'s relatively few transatlantic voyages there was a mutiny aboard. The ship's Sailing Master was a mariner of the old school, named G S Banks. The two leaders of the revolt were armed but Banks strode towards them shouting: 'I'll break you over my knee.' They shot him, twice, but he kept moving and did just that: killed them both with his bare hands, according to his grandson, sailmaker Bill Banks Jr, of Roslyn, NY.

The Civil War in America disrupted things still more for the *Great Eastern* and she made a voyage as a troopship for the British government. In 1863 she did carry as many as 1,114 passengers to New York, but losses continued. She was sold and became a cable-laying ship, doing yeoman service, and making herself best remembered as the 'ship that laid the Atlantic cable'. After more Atlantic voyaging she was laid up. In 1886 she became an exhibition ship, with restaurants, music halls, circus and carnival acts aboard her. Half a million people came to see her in that year but two years later she was sold for scrap. When the scrappers opened her double bottom a skeleton was found and thereafter many claimed that this was the reason for her unfortunate career. Nevertheless, the ship remains to this day the 'most talked-of vessel in the history of steam navigation', in the words of K A Frost.

Gross tonnage: 18,915
Length overall: 689 feet
Width: 82 feet
Machinery: Two oscillating steam engines, one for paddles, one for screw
Speed: 13.5 knots
Capacity: 596 Cabin, 2,400 Steerage (never finished)
Built: J Scott Russell, Milwall, London, 1854-9
Demise: Scrapped in New Ferry, Mersey, England, 1889-91

Thousands of copies of this Currier and Ives print were sold.

Above *An etching by Norman Wilkinson of the huge ship under way done for the* National Geographic Magazine.
Below *A model of the* Great Eastern *showing the full hull and a cut-away of the interior.*

Above *A deck scene—the* Great Eastern. **Below** *Profile and plan published in 1917 in* Scientific American.

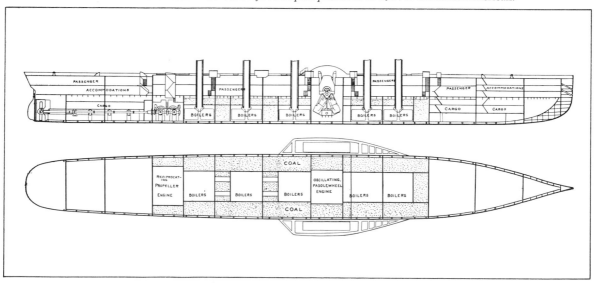

Oregon

It was daybreak on Sunday, March 14 1886. High in his tower on the westernmost end of Fire Island, the lighthouse keeper sighted a huge four-masted, two-stacked steamship about a dozen miles off the beach. She was drifting towards the south-east. He knew that the famous Cunarder *Oregon*, one of the largest ships in the world and the holder of the Atlantic Blue Riband, was due to pass his light about this time heading towards New York. This ship had to be she. He telegraphed Vernon H Brown, Cunard's agent in Manhattan. Without a moment's loss, Mr Brown ordered four tugs to head for the vessel. This was how news of the sinking of the *Oregon* reached New York.

Ships did not have wireless in those days. The *Oregon* had sailed from Liverpool on Saturday, March 6. Aboard were 186 passengers in her ultra-luxurious First Class, 66 travelling Second, and 395 emigrants in Steerage. Her complement numbered 205 officers and crew. The crossing had been uneventful and as Sunday came the ship moved through calm water under a clear night sky. Chief Officer Mathews was on the bridge. Captain Cottier was in his cabin. At 4.20 the ship shuddered—she had been hit by a vessel forward on the port side. Later, the Chief Officer remembered that the other craft had been running without lights. He thought she had been a schooner. There were cries from both vessels and then black silence. A Mrs Hurst from

Brooklyn remembered being awakened by 'a red flash' in her cabin porthole. The damage to the *Oregon* was substantial. Her iron hull was pierced and a hole 'that you could drive a horse and wagon through' was made, in the words of another Brooklyn passenger, John Hopkins.

Unfortunately for the *Oregon*, the blow from the other ship penetrated the liner at her most vulnerable spot. Just below the grand saloon, 65 feet long and 50 feet wide, was the largest of her hull compartments. It was 127 feet long and, if flooded, could hold 3,000 tons of water. With this flooded, watertight doors would not save her. Deck Officer John Huston saw the damage and promptly put over the side some heavy canvas, hoping to make it serve as a collision mat. He and Second Officer John Hood leaped overboard to try to secure the canvas into position. It did not stop the inward surge of green water. On the bridge, Captain Cottier ordered the course changed so the ship could be grounded on Fire Island. But just at this point the *Oregon*'s boilers were being flooded and the black gang abandoned ship. Rockets were sent up and guns fired.

There was no panic among the officers and the passengers were all awakened. They came on deck where coffee and tea were served. Then they were urged back to their cabins for warm clothing. Some

of the frightened black gang seized the lifeboat and pulled away, but there were eight boats remaining and help was in sight. As dawn broke the *Phantom*, pilot boat No 11, came alongside. Also on the scene was the schooner *Fannie A Graham*. Off on the horizon a large passenger liner was approaching. All the passengers were successfully transferred to the two sailing craft. Captain Cottier was the last to leave the big liner, now down by her port bow and sinking fast. She had remained afloat three hours after the impact, a tribute to her good Glasgow construction.

The approaching liner was the *Fulda*, of the North German Lloyd. She arrived in the nick of time for the two smaller rescue craft were dangerously overloaded. A second transfer of passengers and crew took place, again without loss of life. The *Fulda* headed towards New York with 1,700 persons aboard. There were no survivors from the mysterious schooner which had hit the *Oregon*. Her identity has remained a question mark ever since, although the schooner *Charles Morse* was posted missing that night.

This was the end of the *Oregon*'s short and sad career. She was a climax to the dreams of veteran shipping man Stephen Guion, an American who operated out of England. After many years of working for others, including Cunard, he had decided to create his own line. His goal was to have the finest, fastest, and largest ships in the world and, despite some early disappointments, he succeeded. Three remarkable liners were to be the best known and most successful ships in his short-lived company: *Alaska, Arizona,* and *Oregon.* All three were record-breakers in size, speed, and luxury. But company finances were not good: Guion's earlier difficulties, plus the cost of his last three ships, drove him into bankruptcy just as the *Oregon* was establishing her reputation. She broke the speed record for the Atlantic on her maiden voyage in 1883, averaging almost 18 knots, but creditors were pounding on Guion's door and he was forced to sell his newest and finest vessel to his arch-rival—Cunard.

The *Oregon* was lost only two years later, the first major maritime disaster in Cunard's 43-year history. Today, her hulk is well known to American skindivers. The author has a plate brought up from the sandy bottom of the Atlantic by one of these men.

Gross tonnage: 7,375
Length overall: 520 feet
Width: 54 feet
Machinery: Three-cylinder, three-crank compound
Speed: 18.39 knots
Capacity: 340 First, 92 Intermediate, 110 Third, 1,000 Steerage
Build: John Elder & Co, Glasgow, 1883
Demise: Sunk 1886 off Fire Island, NY

Right *An interesting sketch showing the Guion Line pier in Manhattan with the* Oregon's *companion liner, the* Arizona, *about to sail.*

Right *The sinking of the* Oregon *off Fire Island, New York.*

Below right *The* Oregon's *near sister, the* Arizona, *won great acclaim by crashing into an iceberg and surviving.*

Left *The* Oregon *entering New York at the end of her maiden voyage from Queenstown, Ireland, in 1883.*

Oregon

City of Paris

Few liners have had a more auspicious beginning, illustrious career, and sad ending than the *City of Paris*. She and her sister ship, *City of New York*, were twin-screw ships. This was more than just a design refinement. It marked the turning point when shipowners and insurance companies finally became confident enough in the ship's power plant to abandon sails. As built, the *City of Paris* had the traditional three masts of a full-rigged ship, and these were fitted to carry both square and fore-and-aft sails. But her two propeller shafts obviated the need for sail power. In the past, with only one shaft, many steamers had been forced to come in under sail after an accident but now the chances of both shafts breaking were almost nil and sail was doomed. When a ship had to rely on sails, even as a last resort, her superstructure could not be higher than one level of deckhouses. Once sails were abandoned, the tier-on-tier superstructure could evolve. Until the *City of Paris*, all steamships were really auxiliary sailing ships. They had to be able to use sails if necessary. From then on the vestigial remnants of sail became fewer and less obvious.

The *City of Paris* was a beauty. With three stacks, clipper bowsprit, and classic counter stern, she was one of the most graceful of liners—and she was fast: she immediately broke the Atlantic record in both directions. She was not only beautiful and fast, but safe. Frank C Bowen, in his standard work *A Century Of Atlantic Travel,* wrote in 1930 that she and her sister ship 'still have the reputation of being the most perfectly subdivided Atlantic liners ever put afloat.' Their 15 transverse bulkheads were continued 15 feet above the waterline. Below the saloon deck there were no openings in these bulkheads, not even watertight doors.

So much happened to the *City of Paris* that it is hard to tell it all within the bounds permitted by this work. She became a pawn in international finance and was the subject of one of the strangest ownership changes in maritime history. The J P Morgan interests in America were attempting to create a monopoly for themselves by buying up a large number of transatlantic lines. The owners of the *City of Paris* and her sister ship, Inman Line, were already largely financed by Americans and the two crack ships were transferred under a special act of the US Congress to the American flag. This was made possible by an understanding reached by government authorities with the American Line to build two larger ships in an American yard. These were to be the *St Louis* and the *St Paul.* When the two Inman

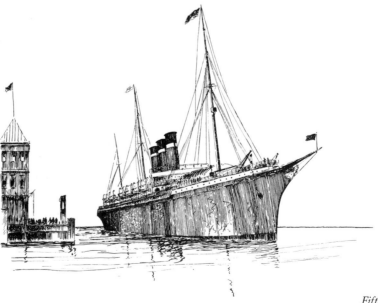

ships came under the Blue Eagle house-flag of the American company, their names were changed to *Paris* and *New York*.

A book should be written on the *Paris* and the *New York*, the last clipper-bowed de luxe liners built for the Atlantic. In the American war with Spain they were pressed into service as armed merchant cruisers, the *Paris* being renamed the *Yale* and the *New York* becoming the *Harvard*. During the *Paris'* period under US Navy control, the three-stacked beauty was actually under fire a number of times off Cuba and replied in kind. Fortunately this indignity did not last long and the vessel was returned to American Line service, only to become victim to another even more awkward moment. A few hours after leaving Southampton, while steaming in dense fog, she ran aground off the Manacles at Land's End, Cornwall. She was held on shore by granite fangs for three weeks, and released only after compressed air had driven the water out of her hull and permitted the holes to be cemented over. It was another turning point in her glittering career.

She was towed to Belfast and rebuilt. Her name was again changed, this time to *Philadelphia*. Her three superb funnels were removed and in their place two taller ones were installed. She looked terrible. Worse still, her middle mast was removed some time later, completely destroying her finely proportioned silhouette. Nevertheless she served most successfully for the next two decades until America entered World War 1. This was a period of tremendous change in Atlantic liner design and by virtually every yardstick except speed and safety the clipper-bowed sea queens were left far behind. In 1917 she became the American troop ship, *Harrisburg*. She steamed 270,000 miles during the war, landing 30,000 troops in France under the command of Commodore Henry A Candy. After the Armistice she brought many of the survivors home.

The final sad chapter in her life began when she was bought in 1922 by the New York-Naples Steamship Co and set out on a voyage to Constantinople. Her last stop was her first on this debacle— Naples. Her owners were bankrupt, her crew mutinous, and the authorities arrested everyone they could find aboard and threw them into a rat-infested prison. She became an abandoned hulk, drifted ashore, and was finally sold for scrap, towed to Genoa and demolished.

Gross tonnage: 10,499 (1889), 10,508 (1893), 10,786 (1899)
Length overall: 560 feet
Width: 63 feet
Machinery: Steam triple-expansion engines geared to twin screw
Speed: 20 knots
Capacity: 540 First, 200 Second, 1,000 Steerage (1889); 290 First, 250 Second, 725 Steerage (1893); Second and Steerage only (1913)
Built: Thomson Shipyards, Glasgow, Scotland, 1889
Demise: Broken up in Genoa, Italy, 1923

An interesting painting showing the City of Paris *on her first arrival in New York under the American flag. Note the 'Blue Eagle' house-flag of the American Line on the foremast.*

City of Paris

Above *A replica of an original drawing of the* City of New York, *sister ship of the* City of Paris. *Note in the cut-away below that fore-and-aft sails are set.*

Below *During the Spanish-American War the* Paris *was repainted in grey as the armed merchant cruiser USS* Yale.

Fifty Famous Liners

Above *The 560-foot long vessel aground off the Manacles, Land's End, Cornwall.*
Below *Renamed the* Philadelphia, *she was rebuilt with two considerably taller funnels and, still later, lost her middlemast as well.*

Oceanic

Although the *Oceanic* of 1899 would live only 15 years, and although she was surpassed in speed, size and elegance while she was still virtually new, this stately liner will always have a special place and prominence in Atlantic liner history. There was something about her, something that no other liner before or since had, something that set her apart. Could it have been her two very tall and perfectly raked smokestacks? Surely no other ship has ever had such a pair of perfectly proportioned funnels so widely spaced? Perhaps it might have been her three pole masts, or the great length or seemingly great length of her beautifully designed forecastle? Maybe it was her overall sleekness of outline? Or perhaps it was the combination of all these special features? She was, without doubt, a dream ship.

When new in 1899 she was described as 'the greatest and most elaborately fitted vessel ever constructed'. Thomas H Ismay, founder of the White Star Line which owned her, looked at the *Oceanic* as the ultimate ship of his career. He saw her launched and then went into a rapid physical decline, passing away just before her completion. The *Oceanic* was the first ship to exceed the *Great Eastern* in length, although her 17,272 gross tons were slightly less than the 18,915 of the much earlier vessel. She was to have been the first of a pair of White Star express liners, her sister ship to be called *Olympic*. There was some talk of calling her *Gigantic* but this never happened and her sister was never built, the name *Olympic* being reserved for later use.

Luxury and elegance were words that had continuously been used for each new flagship, but never were they more appropriate than with the *Oceanic*. Her dining saloon for First Class could seat more than 400 and was topped by a 21-foot square dome. It was illuminated in part by light from two rows of oversized portholes, one on either side of the ship's hull. She had 2,000 electric lamps aboard. Her library, thought by many to be her most beautiful public room, was not unlike the very posh library on the modern-day *France/Norway*. She could carry 410 in First, 300 in Second, and 1,000 in Third Class and served on the route from Liverpool to Queenstown to New York.

The *Oceanic* was a fast ship, averaging 18.96 knots under reduced power on her maiden voyage, but she never broke the record. She began the White Star tradition of having large and comfortable ships instead of record-breakers. In rapid succession she was followed by the famous 'Big Four' of the Atlantic: *Celtic, Cedric, Baltic,* and *Adriatic.* Each of these was larger than the *Oceanic.* They were also considerably slower, leading many to conjure that the *Oceanic* had been planned as a record-breaker,

but for one reason or another—possibly vibration—did not make it.

Although surpassed in size by others in her own fleet, and in speed by German and British rivals, the *Oceanic* remained the crack ship of White Star until the *Olympic* was put into service in 1911. She regularly made 20-knot crossings and was highly popular with many sophisticated passengers, notably J Pierpont Morgan, who at this time had become her owner. His efforts to create a monopoly of the transatlantic liner business were only partially successful at the time of his death in 1913.

The normal number of collisions, accidents, and fires happened with the *Oceanic*, but J Bruce Ismay was sure to see that she was quickly repaired in each case and kept in tip-top condition, as she had been the last liner launched in his father's lifetime. An unusual incident took place in 1911 when the liner was struck by lightning: it hit her foremast and the whole ship felt the impact; a nine-foot mast fragment crashed down on deck sending splinters all over the open bridge and barely missing the glass dome over the library; the ship's wireless was put out of commission for a short time.

When the *Titanic* sailed in early 1912, the suction from her motion pulled the *Oceanic* out from her berth so far that a 60-foot gangway linking her to her pier fell into the sea. So rapid had been the evolution of the liner between 1899 and 1912 that the *Titanic*, 46,328 tons, made the *Oceanic* look small, although the two were not so much different in length. It would be the older ship's fate to pick up a lifeboat from her new companion ship only days later, a boat in which were found three bodies so badly decomposed that they had to be buried at sea on the spot.

The *Oceanic*'s end was sudden and sad. Taken over by the Navy, she was put under the command of a naval officer not experienced in the ways of large merchant ships. Her regular master was demoted to second-in-command. She was wrecked in bad weather on Foula Island, in the Shetlands, and disappeared beneath the waves two weeks later.

Gross tonnage: 17,272
Length overall: 704 feet
Width: 63 feet
Machinery: Steam triple-expansion engines geared to twin screw
Speed: 20 knots
Capacity: 410 First, 300 Second, 1,000 Steerage
Built: Harland & Wolff Ltd, Belfast, Northern Ireland, 1899
Demise: Stranded in fog in the Shetland Islands, September 8 1914; scrapped under the water by 1924

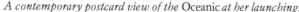

A contemporary postcard view of the Oceanic *at her launching.*

A Modern Liner.   Afloat.

Left *Maiden arrival in New York.*

Below *Leaving New York after one of her first visits in 1899.*

Right *Heading out to sea past Staten Island in 1899—the gallant* Oceanic.

Below right *A tug comes alongside the* Oceanic.

Fifty Famous Liners

Virginian

The British-flag passenger ship, *Virginian*, belongs to a unique group in the world fleet. She survived to her fiftieth birthday. This was made even more outstanding in that she spent very little time idle. She was notable both at the beginning of her life and in the years near her end. She and her sister ship, *Victorian*, were, in 1905, the first turbine-driven ocean steamships. In 1954, as the *Homeland*, she was by far the oldest liner on the transatlantic run.

The *Virginian* and the *Victorian* were commissioned as part of the Allan Line for service between Liverpool and St John, New Brunswick, during the winter and along the St Lawrence to Montreal in the ice-free summer season. They were actually quite revolutionary in that they could reach the East Coast of Canada from Liverpool in just under six days, which was considerably ahead of all other passenger ships on that very northern run. The accommodation was divided as 470 First Class, 240 Second, and 940 Steerage. Both ships were highly successful, particularly as the Steerage quarters were filled with new settlers on most westbound voyages.

The *Virginian* was requisitioned for war duty on November 13 1914, for use as a troop transport for the Canadian Expeditionary Force. Shortly thereafter, she was converted to an Armed Merchant Cruiser and assigned to the Tenth Cruiser Squadron. She served well, with an accident-free record, until 'paying-off' on December 7 1917. Another year

passed before, on December 23, she docked at Glasgow for a thorough refit and restoration for commercial operations. The refit progressed but near the end she was declared surplus to Canadian Pacific Steamships, the new owners of the original Allan Line. The *Virginian* did not hoist the Canadian Pacific house-flag but was offered for sale. Almost immediately, she was sold to the Swedish American Line. She completed her overhaul on January 31 1920 and left the British Register on February 14.

Her Swedish owners were in desperate need of tonnage, especially to transport the thousands of Swedes seeking passage to America and Canada. She was renamed *Drottningholm*, honouring Drottningholm Castle, which is so lavish as to be known as the 'Versailles of the North'. There was a brief period spent in dry dock with few alterations except that her berthing plans now read: 426 First Class, 286 Second, and 1,000 Third Class. In May of 1920, she departed from Gothenburg on her maiden crossing to New York and thereafter was paired with the *Stockholm*, a ship dating from 1900 and formerly Holland-America's *Potsdam*.

Drottningholm underwent some changes during an extended annual overhaul in 1922. Her original turbines were replaced by newer ones of De Laval design, which would keep her speed at just over 19 knots. The accommodation was again changed as well. The arrangement now read: 532 Cabin Class

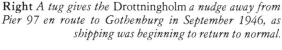

Right *A tug gives the* Drottningholm *a nudge away from Pier 97 en route to Gothenburg in September 1946, as shipping was beginning to return to normal.*

Virginian

and 854 Third Class. More accurately, she joined a transatlantic group of passenger vessels known as 'cabin liners'.

One passenger described her interiors as similar to those of a 'mellow old country inn'. Although she was a notorious roller, this somehow added to the sense of cosiness and charm. There was a glass-enclosed verandah, music lounge, garden lounge, and a smoking room highlighted by a glass-vaulted quarter-dome with a sixteenth-century ship motif. Only four of her staterooms had private bathrooms, and there were two de luxe cabins with twin cane beds and sitting alcoves.

Possibly the *Drottningholm*'s most famous passenger came aboard in the early summer of 1925. When the ship docked at New York's Pier 97 on July 6, several reporters went aboard to photograph a very young and very shy Swedish actress who was being lured to the United States by the offer of a small Hollywood contract—her name: Greta Garbo.

The hull was repainted in white during 1932 and the ship began to make occasional cruises from New York. She became quite popular on cruises from Gothenburg to the North Cape, into the Baltic and along the Mediterranean. However, most of the cruise services were run by the larger and newer *Kungsholm* and *Gripsholm*. The *Drottningholm* maintained the transatlantic service, even in frigid winter months.

At the outbreak of World War 2, the *Drottningholm* was designated a 'mercy ship'. Her purpose was to carry diplomats, displaced persons, and exchange prisoners, and she was to be free of any attack. She flew special flags, had large signs painted along her sides, and had a highly visible illuminated sign for travelling at night. She was used by the International Red Cross for repatriation work on far-flung voyages that took her to such areas as Turkey, India, and North Africa. On one sailing to Istanbul, she carried representatives from 39 different countries.

She survived her second war but was almost immediately sold to the newly formed Home Lines of Panama, a company in which Swedish-American had substantial financial interests. However, the transfer was postponed for nearly three years, until 1948, when the new motorliner, *Stockholm*, could adequately replace the older ship.

The last Swedish-American sailing for the *Drottningholm* took place on February 13 1948, from New York to Gothenburg. It was her 440th voyage wherein she had carried 192,000 transatlantic passengers and 11,300 on cruises. Little time was spared. She joined her new owners, was renamed *Brasil*, and left Genoa for South America with a capacity load of immigrants on April 8. Another highly successful phase had begun.

During 1950, which was a Roman Catholic Holy Year, she was back on the North Atlantic, trading between Genoa, Naples, and New York. A major refit followed during the next winter. She was altered to carry 96 First Class and 846 Tourist Class passengers, and was given her fourth and last name, *Homeland.* In June of 1951, she began sailing between Hamburg, the Channel ports, and New York, but in the following year went back to the Mediterranean. The end came in February 1955. She was sold to SIDARMA, an Italian scrap firm, and docked at Trieste on March 29. Her fiftieth year was her last.

Gross tonnage: 10,754
Length overall: 538 feet
Width: 60 feet
Machinery: Steam turbines geared to triple screw
Speed: 18 knots
Capacity: 470 First, 240 Second, 940 Steerage
Built: Alexander Stephen & Sons Limited, Glasgow, Scotland, 1905
Demise: Scrapped in Trieste, Italy, 1955

Above right *The Swedish-American liner* Drottningholm *sailing up the Hudson River to her dock in Jersey City bringing diplomats, newspapermen and others from Germany and Italy to a safe America.*
Right *The hull of the* Drottningholm *was repainted white in 1932 and the ship began occasional cruises from New York.*

The promenade garden lounge aboard the Drottningholm.

The bar on the Drottningholm.

The smoking room on the Drottningholm.

Kronprinzessin Cecilie

The transatlantic run at the turn of the century was in one of its busiest periods. Steamship firms and whole nations were competing, particularly for the glorious distinctions of biggest, longest, and fastest ocean queens. More exactly, the race was on between Britain and Germany. If government ministers and shipping-board members could enthusiastically justify their lavish and often costly constructions, so could the vast numbers that would sail in these ships. It was an age of unrestricted immigration to the United States and each of these vessels had a Third or Steerage Class that reflected this. Although there was increasingly imaginative luxury in the First Class quarters, the real earning-power of these liners was in the Steerage Classes. These passengers, who might have paid as little as £6 10s for their crossing, were given the least amount of space on board, yet often constituted the largest number. They travelled throughout the year, regardless of season and the furies of the Atlantic, for the 'voyage of a lifetime'.

The North German Lloyd and the Hamburg America Line were the principal German companies, stemming from the port cities of Bremen and Hamburg respectively, and with a strong sense of competitiveness even between themselves. North German's four-funnel *Kaiser Wilhelm der Grosse* was launched as the world's largest liner (14,300 tons, 655 feet long) in May 1897. A few months later, in September, she crossed to New York and captured the Blue Riband from Britain's *Lucania* of Cunard. At a recorded 22.35 knots, she was the first German ship to do this and opened a new era.

Not to be outdone, Hamburg America launched the 16,500-ton *Deutschland* in 1900. She immediately took the Riband. A year later, in September, the third of the Germanic four-stackers set out on her maiden run. She was the 14,900-ton *Kronprinz Wilhelm*, owned by the North German Lloyd. Then, there were refinements to that design which led to the 19,300-ton *Kaiser Wilhelm II*, delivered in March 1903. Just as with the earlier ships, her performance only encouraged the Germans to continue further, although with a sister ship rather an evolutionary larger liner. Just as the *Kaiser Wilhelm II* was taking the Riband in the summer of 1906, the steel frames for her sister were being set in place at the Vulcan yards in Stettin.

The construction moved quickly, just as the Atlantic trade continued to flourish. The launch took place on December 1 1906, and the new liner followed the naming policy of honouring the German imperial family—the honour befell Princess Cecilia of Prussia, the daughter of Crown Prince Wilhelm.

The brand new *Kronprinzessin Cecilie* left Bremerhaven for New York on August 6 1907, just at the time that Germany was to forfeit the cherished Blue Riband, held for 22 years, to the British *Mauretania*. There were no record runs for the newest North German four-stacker but she still represented one of the Atlantic's finest passenger ships. Her full capacity of 1,808 plus 602 crew was not unusually high for the era, yet included a high standard First Class and a bold advertisement towards 'greatly improved' Third Class quarters. Her 19,300 tons and 707 feet were quite impressive, making her one of the Atlantic's mightiest ships, but the actual distinction of 'world's largest' had gone also to Britain, to the afore-mentioned *Mauretania* and her sister *Lusitania*. No matter how remotely, Germany's liners seemed to have lost their ability to compete successfully, at least for the time being. It was not until 1913 that Hamburg America's *Imperator* was listed as the largest afloat. However, distinctive in some quarters, the new *Kronprinzessin Cecilie* had the largest steam reciprocating machinery ever fitted to a ship.

The foursome—*Kaiser Wilhelm der Grosse, Kronprinz Wilhelm, Kaiser Wilhelm II,* and *Kronprinzessin Cecilie*—prospered over the following years and made a most colourful set, each with its great mustard-coloured stacks. The fifth of this four-funnel group, Hamburg America's *Deutschland*, suffered mechanical and vibration problems and was finally converted to a cruise ship in 1910. But the age of the German four-stacker was over. North German Lloyd added the *George Washington*, larger still at 25,500 tons, in 1909 with the revised silhouette of four masts and two thin stacks.

The *Kronprinzessin Cecilie* was at sea, on July 29 1914, bound for Europe, when news was received of the imminent outbreak of war. Frighteningly, she was carrying, in addition to some German passengers and other valued cargo, some $10,000,000 in gold bars and a further $1,000,000 in silver. Her captain realised that she could never hope to reach Bremerhaven without risking capture. Instead, a rather elaborate scheme was offered. He ordered that lights should be extinguished and the wireless shut down. Some passengers were furious at the mysterious escapade, others were delighted to be part of the adventure, while yet another group offered to buy the ship so that she could hoist American colours for safety! The tops of the four funnels were given black bands in an effort to disguise the ship as the British *Olympic* of White Star Line. The course was reversed and the so-called 'German treasure-ship' headed for the neutral waters of the United States. On August 4, much to the surprise of the local residents, the liner appeared in the tiny bay of Bar Harbor, Maine. Word spread quickly that the *Olympic*, the famed sister of the *Titanic*, was for some reason anchored alongside the customary yachts and sailing boats. Although the ship's true identity was quickly uncovered, she had successfully escaped the war.

The *Kronprinzessin Cecilie* spent several months at Bar Harbor, under the command of her German Captain, but then, once America entered the hostilities, she was towed to Boston. She was seized by the United States Navy, outfitted as a transport and began sailing as the USS *Mount Vernon* in April 1917. Because of her heritage, American servicemen who sailed in her referred to the ship as the 'Vermin'. Misfortune struck on September 5 1918 when she was torpedoed 200 miles off Brest. Somehow, she managed to remain afloat but there was an exact hit on the boiler room and 36 perished. She was finally towed into port, temporarily repaired, and then recrossed the Atlantic, only to be laid up.

By 1919, the German four-stackers were all but gone. The *Kaiser Wilhelm der Grosse* was scuttled in 1914. The *Deutschland* was rebuilt as the immigrant ship, *Hansa*, had two of her funnels removed and then was scrapped by 1925. The *Kronprinz Wilhelm*, interned at Newport News, Virginia, in 1915, was used briefly by the Americans as the transport USS *Von Steuben* before being scrapped in

1923. The final pair were handed over to the United States Shipping Board in 1920, but without much further hope.

A serious proposal was put forth by designer William Francis Gibbs, who supervised the restoration of the *Leviathan* and later designed the superb *America* and brilliant *United States*, that called for the *Mount Vernon* (ex-*Kronprinzessin Cecilie*) and the *Agamemnon* (ex-*Kaiser Wilhelm II*) to be converted to diesel drive and thoroughly renovated for the transatlantic passenger trade under the US flag. There were a variety of problems, including financial ones, and the project was ultimately abandoned. Both ships were sent to Chesapeake Bay and laid up.

In 1940, there was a glimmer of hope. The 34-year-old former *Kronprinzessin Cecilie*—after 21 years of idleness and neglect—was offered to Great Britain for use as a trooper. The necessary repairs and alterations would have been too costly and thus the offer was declined. Instead, both she and her former sister were sold to the Boston Iron & Metal Company and broken up in Baltimore, by which time Germany was again at war.

Gross tonnage: 19,360
Length overall: 707 feet
Width: 72 feet
Machinery: Quadruple expansion engines geared to twin screw
Speed: 23 knots
Capacity: 742 First, 326 Second, 740 Steerage
Built: A G Vulcan, Stettin, Germany, 1907
Demise: Scrapped in Baltimore, Maryland, 1940

Fifty Famous Liners

Above *The* Kronprinzessin Cecile *with her paired stacks standing out against lower Manhattan's skyline.*

Below *The sleek German speed queen entering Bar Harbor, Maine, USA, disguised as a White Star liner at the outbreak of the Great War.*

Left *Converted into a US transport and renamed* Mt Vernon, *the four-stacker is dry-docked for hull-painting.*

Below *After her war service the* Mt Vernon *is laid up.*

Right *In 1924 she is towed from Boston, Massachusetts, to a permanent lay-up site in the James River, Virginia.*

Below right *Four former German liners in the James River Reserve Fleet. From left to right: the* George Washington, *the* America *(ex* Amerika*), the* Agamemnon *(ex* Monticello, *ex* Kaiser Wilhelm II*) and the* Mt Vernon *(ex* Kronprinzessin Cecilie*)* (Courtesy Steamship Historical Society of America).

U.S.S. MOUNT VERNON

Kronprinzessin Cecilie   37

Lusitania

'The Lusitania proves beyond a reasonable doubt that the British government connived at the sinking of the passenger ship in order to lure America into World War I,' wrote the *Los Angeles Times* when reviewing the latest of the many books about this historic and tragic ship. The chief thesis of Colin Simpson's work, entitled simply *The Lusitania*, is that the German submarine which torpedoed the great four-stacker was an unwitting partner in a plot that was in all probability concocted by Winston Churchill.

With such an albatross hanging around her neck, how can the *Lusitania* be dealt with properly in a book such as this? Let us state at the start that were history entirely different, had she not been sunk and in effect brought the United States into the war, the *Lusitania* would still have been included in this work. She was, in her own right, one of the great liners of all time—without question, a milestone in maritime history.

In a sense the *Lusitania* was a result of the attempt by American millionaire, J P Morgan, to create for himself a monopoly of the Atlantic liner business. Starting in 1902, he purchased first this and then that company, sending waves of outrage throughout Europe, particularly England. Finally, when the great White Star Line was bought by Morgan, the British Parliament acted. Cunard Line, which might well have been absorbed, was given a 20-year contract which, in return for a pledge to remain strictly British, provided incentives to build the two largest and fastest ships in the world. They became

the *Lusitania* and the *Mauretania*. Being the first, the *Lusitania* won most of the early laurels—and no ship deserved them more. Cunard had thought hard and well about what engines to use for their new record-breakers, and in 1905 the decision was made. It was based on two fine 20,000-ton ships of identical design, put into service that year. One had an old-style reciprocating power plant and the other was turbine powered. The *Caronia*, with her quadruple-expansion engines, made 19.7 knots on her trials with a freshly painted, clean hull. Her turbine-driven sister, *Carmania*, averaged almost a knot more and with a dirty hull. The new greyhounds would be turbine powered. Their statistics were the subject of countless articles and the shipping world was left gasping by such facts as that the new sisters would each require 4,000,000 rivets and that they would have 175 watertight compartments and be as unsinkable as a ship could be. Each would cost £1,250,000, or nearly double what the *Oceanic* had cost. They would consume 840 tons of coal per day and, to this, diehards noted that equal speed could have been obtained with less fuel consumption had reciprocating engines been selected.

A principal goal for the *Lusitania* was to wrest back the speed record from Germany. Like the German speed queens she was to have four stacks, but Cunard's naval architects showed their independence by refusing to go along with the German style of having two sets of paired smokestacks. There have been only 14 four-stacked ocean liners built in all time and the first five were all

An interesting stern view of the liner arriving in New York.

German, with paired funnels. The *Lusitania* broke this tradition by having her stacks evenly spaced. Whereas the 17,000-ton *Oceanic* had been the largest ship in the world in 1899, only eight years later the *Lusitania* would pass the 30,000-ton mark for the first time in marine history. She had originally been announced as being of 28,000 gross tons, but when put on her trials in the summer of 1907 she was measured at 31,550 tons. Three German twin-screw liners in a row had held the transatlantic speed record over a decade before her. The *Lusitania* won it on her second westward passage with an average of 23.993 knots and a best day's run of 617 miles. She and her sister were the first quadruple-screw record-breakers.

In looks, the *Lusitania* and later her sister set new standards of ocean liner beauty. From their sleek, straight stems to their beautifully rounded bridges, and their long, low superstructures capped by their four smokestacks, racily raked, to their sleek and aristocratic counter sterns, they were a naval architect's dream come true. The *Lusitania* differed from the *Mauretania* in appearance primarily because of lower, less evident air funnels—her stacks seemed taller.

The twin beauties took turns at breaking each other's Atlantic records. The *Lusitania* was the first to average more than 25 knots, with a best day's run of 643 miles at 25.43 knots. Soon, both were over the 26-knot average point and they continued to cut each other's records by a minute here and a minute there—amazing, wonderful performances by both.

The war destroyed all this and so much more. Its long range impact on history has yet to be properly understood. The part the *Lusitania* was to play had nothing to do with her qualities as a great ship. She was the victim of the war, as were the millions who were slaughtered in that asinine display of mankind's stupidity.

Gross tonnage: 31,550
Length overall: 787 feet
Width: 87 feet
Machinery: Steam turbines geared to quadruple screw
Speed: 25 knots
Capacity: 563 First, 464 Second, 1,138 Third
Built: John Brown & Company Limited, Clydebank, Scotland, 1907
Demise: Torpedoed and sunk off the Irish coast, May 7 1915

Left *The great Cunarder* Lusitania *arriving at New York's Pier 54, at the foot of West 12th Street, on her 1907 maiden voyage.*

Right *Port-side boat deck.*

Below *Leaving New York in early 1915. Across the Hudson at the Hoboken docks (left to right) are several laid-up German liners including the* Vaterland, *the four-funnel* Kronprinz Wilhelm, *and the* George Washington. *In the centre are the* Rotterdam *and the* Potsdam *of Holland-America.*

Mauretania

She was the most famous and sought-after liner of her day—with a popularity and acclaim that ranged from European royalty, to businessmen from San Francisco, to immigrant labourers from Wales. She was the epitome of engineering genius—the fastest ship in the world. She brought honours to her country, snatching them back from rival Germany. She was sleek, mighty, and majestic, and influenced the design of all future ocean queens. Even in her later years—her twilight—she was still well respected and known fondly as the 'Dowager of the Atlantic'.

The British government was quite unhappy with the supreme position held by the Germans at the turn-of-the-century on the North Atlantic, and was further aggravated by the sale of their White Star Line to the Morgan financial interests of America. Honours and corporate safety had to be re-established and so the government voted a £2.6 million construction loan for the Cunard Line, then the dominant English transatlantic firm. In addition, there was a £150,000 annual mail subsidy, given on condition that Cunard remained British for a minimum of 20 years and did not sell out to American investors.

The result of this arrangement was not only the largest pair of liners in the world (they were finally outstepped in 1911 by White Star's *Olympic*), but the most powerful afloat. They were the first major ships to be fitted with steam turbines, which had developed to the point of being vastly superior to the earlier steam reciprocating engines. On board the ships, named *Lusitania* (for Roman Portugal) and *Mauretania* (for Roman Morocco), there were 25 boilers and 192 furnaces, a storage capacity for 6,000 tons of coal with a reserve in the second cargo hold, all of which produced a service speed between 24 and 25 knots. This represented a consumption of 1,000 tons of coal per day.

While the *Lusitania* is listed under a separate section, her sister was ordered from the Newcastle firm of Swan, Hunter & Wigham Richardson

Right *The* Mauretania *undocking (a tugman's term for 'sailing') with the* Paris *preceding her down the Hudson to the sea.*

Mauretania

Limited in May 1905, and was launched a year later, on September 20, the ceremony being performed by the Dowager Duchess of Roxburgh. Even at her launch, she was a large ship, at a total of 16,800 tons. Her trials—run in the autumn of 1907—were wonderfully recorded, showing an unheard-of average of 26.3 knots. The *Mauretania* was accepted by Cunard with the greatest joy. On November 16 1907, she left Liverpool on her maiden crossing to New York, a trip heralded as Britain's new golden age in Atlantic shipping. Together, for the next four years, the *Lusitania* and *Mauretania* sailed unchallenged.

The interiors were highly stylized and represented the glories of great British and European design. The forests of both England and France were scoured for the most perfect woods, some of which were exquisitely carved into great detail. The decor ranged from French Renaissance to English Country and included lavish lounges, smoking rooms, libraries, private parlours, and even a more exotic Palm Court. All of the bathroom fixtures in First Class were silver plated, while those in Second and Third Class were done in what was then striking white metals. A week's crossing in First Class could cost as much as £200 while Steerage might be as low as £20.

The *Mauretania* triumphantly captured the Blue Riband from her sister *Lusitania* on her return, eastbound, maiden voyage in 1907. She had done 23.69 knots between New York's Ambrose Light-

ship and Queenstown, Ireland, as opposed to the *Lusitania*'s 23.61. The twin Cunarders had taken the record from Germany's *Kaiser Wilhelm II*, which had established a record of 23.58 in 1906. This race of speed continued among Europe's great maritime nations for the next three decades.

While the *Mauretania* already had the highly prized Riband, her owners stressed further improvement. During her overhaul in early 1909, she was fitted with a new set of propellers, each having four blades. Consequently, in March of that same year, an astounding record was listed of 25.5 knots, with the best day's run being 671 miles. In June, she averaged 25.8 knots. Then, in September, it finally stood at 26.6 knots. This record average remained unsurpassed until the *Bremen*'s maiden voyage in the summer of 1929, and symbolized Britain's maritime might for over 20 years.

The service between Liverpool and New York was interrupted in the summer of 1914 at the outbreak of war in Europe and was replaced by an irregular service to Halifax. The *Mauretania* was finally coloured in grey and redesignated for trooping. Early in 1915, she made three full voyages to Gallipoli. Later, in September, with her sister by then torpedoed and sunk off Ireland, the *Mauretania* was repainted in the red and white colours of a war-time hospital ship and, among others, made a heroic voyage from the Mediterranean to England with 6,298 wounded aboard.

In 1916, she was transferred back to trooping and was disguised with 'dazzle paint', a system of geometric shapes of various shades of grey that allowed her to blend with the sea and escape the treacherous U-boats. To the mostly American and Canadian servicemen who came on board, she was affectionately dubbed the 'Maury'.

She was back in commercial service on the Atlantic route in 1919, sailing from Southampton rather than Liverpool. Later, she was part of Cunard's 'Big Three'—the Atlantic express trio—which provided weekly sailings in each direction. The *Berengaria* was the flagship; the *Aquitania* was considered the most beautiful; and the *Mauretania* was still the world's fastest. The post-war era had changed the North Atlantic. The American Quota System was established in 1921 and vastly curtailed the once lucrative 'Steerage' business. At the same time, oil as a fuel was rapidly replacing coal. In the early 1920s, the infamous stokers—'the black gangs', as they were called—were fast disappearing from the major ocean liners.

The *Mauretania* was saved from a serious fire in Southampton, on July 25 1921, but the repairs necessitated a return to her builder's yard in Newcastle. Cunard decided to use the occasion for the great ship's transformation to an oil burner and to adjust the passenger accommodation to more contemporary patterns. Her berthing figures were changed therefore from 560 to 589 in First Class, from 475 to 400 in Second Class, and from 1,300 to 767 in Third Class. In addition, she could sail in winter months with 500 or so American millionaires on extended de luxe cruises to the Mediterranean.

Life for the *Mauretania* during the 1920s reflected her continued popularity. She made her first cruise in February 1923, and in 1926 logged an impressive 26.16 knots during an eastbound Atlantic crossing. But faster and much larger liners were taking shape on drawing boards. Even Cunard was planning for the future with a new two-ship transatlantic weekly express service.

The *Mauretania* lost her illustrious Blue Riband record to the 51,000-ton *Bremen* in July 1929. This German successor was a sleek, almost monster-like vessel that registered 27.92 knots against the old Cunarder's 27.22. There were valiant efforts on the part of the *Mauretania*'s crew, which included the tossing of some furniture into the boilers to raise additional steam, but the new liner proved the faster. Congratulations were radioed from the *Mauretania*'s bridge.

Once the Depression had begun, the Atlantic passenger trade slowly began to dwindle. Beginning in 1930, the *Mauretania* was sent mostly on cruises, to Havana and Kingston, Villefranche and Naples. In 1932, she was given a white hull, which added a tropical flavour and which denoted her year-round use as a cruise liner thereafter. The end came in September 1934. She left New York for the last time on the same day (September 26) that the *Queen Mary* was being launched in Clydebank, Scotland. This new ship was to succeed and become the world's fastest liner.

The *Mauretania* was laid up at first along the Southampton docks. She was a perfect candidate for a floating museum, but was instead sold off in the spring of the following year to ship-breakers in Rosyth in Scotland. She is still considered to be one of the greatest liners of the twentieth century. Her record survives.

Gross tonnage: 31,938 (1907), 30,696 (1921)
Length overall: 790 feet
Width: 88 feet
Machinery: Steam turbines geared to quadruple screw
Speed: 25 knots
Capacity: 560 First, 475 Second, 1,300 Third (1907); 589 First, 400 Second, 767 Third (1921)
Built: Swan, Hunter & Wigham Richardson Limited, Newcastle, England, 1907
Demise: Scrapped in Rosyth, Scotland, 1935

The camouflaged Mauretania *bringing US troops home from World War 1.*

The magnificent four stacks of the Mauretania *were a favourite subject for ship news photographers of her day.*

Fifty Famous Liners

Mauretania

Above *All white in cruising dress. An aerial view made in 1933.*
Below *Bidders for her furnishings crowd the* Mauretania's *A Deck lounge before her scrapping in 1935.*

Fifty Famous Liners

George Washington

The selection of the name *George Washington* in 1908 for Germany's largest passenger liner may at first seem rather strange. The new ship's purpose was to be a large and luxurious answer for the North German Lloyd to the already existing fleets of the Hamburg America, Cunard, and White Star companies. There would be no question as to the extreme comforts of the day that would be provided for the first-class passengers, but as the firm's directors well realised, the true profits would come from the immigrants in Steerage Class. If not in matters of decor or extensive facilities, the line paid much attention to those passengers who would be travelling in that lowest class. Consequently, the name choice was made as something of a lure to those Germans crossing the Atlantic to become new Americans. Further reflecting this scheme, there were assorted other German liners of the period with such names as *President Lincoln, President Grant, Amerika, Cincinnati,* and *Cleveland.*

The *George Washington* was North German Lloyd's largest ship when she was launched on November 10 1908, at the Vulcan Shipyards in Stettin. Construction efforts were especially accelerated so that the new ship would be christened in that year, the Lloyd's fiftieth anniversary. She was completed by the following June and left Bremerhaven on the twelfth for her maiden crossing to New York. She was well publicised, particularly for her balance of 2,679 passengers and 13,000 tons of cargo. Unlike the other large Atlantic liners of the time, she had two tall, rather thin funnels nestling between four masts, the number of which reminded many of the ships of the later years of the nineteenth century. 'The Big George' prospered, carrying the anticipated thousands of immigrants blended with that more genteel clientele in First Class. The rival Hamburg America Line turned its attention to even bigger liners, namely the 52,000-ton *Imperator,* which would have her debut in 1913. The North German Lloyd was not quite as enthusiastic and selected to move forward from the *George Washington*'s 25,000 tons to a pair of 34,000-ton sisters that were to be called *Columbus* and *Hindenburg.* But the plan was ruinously interrupted by the outbreak of war in the summer of 1914.

Along with ships such as the *Imperator,* the *George Washington* was at her Hoboken pier, just across from Manhattan, and interned for the duration of the hostilities by the United States government. Three years later, in April 1917, as the US entered the war, she was formally seized and transferred to the operations of the American Navy. Repainted in military grey, she began trading on the North Atlantic war-time shuttle. By 1919, she was handed over to the US Army for management, just in time to carry President Wilson and his suite to and from the Versailles Conference. The President came aboard in March and made a return sailing in August. Also in that same year, Their Majesties King Albert and Queen Elisabeth of Belgium used the ship for their visit to the United States.

The ship was laid up in Boston in January 1920, and once again transferred, to the United States Shipping Board. Thought was given to her future and like most other ex-German liners she would not be returned to her original owners. By October, she was chartered to the newly formed United States Mail Lines and sent to the Tietjen and Lang Shipyards in Hoboken for renovation to a luxury passenger ship. It was decided that her popular name would be kept, despite some resentment concerning

its German origin. With her tonnage reduced by nearly 2,000 to 23,788, she left New York for Bremerhaven on August 3 1921, just as the owners were renamed more simply the United States Lines. Briefly thereafter, the *George Washington* found herself sailing in company with an assortment of former German liners, namely the giant *Vaterland*, which was renamed *Leviathan*, and the *Amerika*, restyled with the more obvious spelling of *America*. Even the old *President Grant* of Hamburg America was about, under US colours as the *Republic*.

The *George Washington* was again quite popular and her standard of luxury and comfort was such that she was sent cruising in the off-season. In the winter of 1924, she was heavily advertised as 'the world's ninth largest liner' as she set sail on a de luxe Mediterranean cruise with 150 millionaires aboard.

When the Depression arrived, the 'old George' was among the first casualties. By November 1931, she had been sent to the Patuxent River, in Chesapeake Bay, and laid up until 'better times'. Unfortunately, there was no further encouragement except for a rumour in 1935 that she was to become an American merchant marine training ship.

Unlike the former *Kronprinzessin Cecilie* and *Kaiser Wilhelm II* which were laid up alongside her, the *George Washington* was reactivated with military intentions in 1940. She was again under the jurisdiction of the American Navy and was classified as a transport. A year later, she was transferred to the hard-pressed British Ministry of Transport, renamed *Catlin*, only to be returned to the United States before the year was out. Her age and poor condition made her a difficult and undesirable ship, and she was handed back to the Federal Maritime Commission in February 1942. Examinations revealed that the 33-year-old boilers were well worn. However, this fact was not fully realised by all concerned until she could barely log 11 knots during a series of New York–Panama Canal sailings in the following June. She had to be withdrawn, despite the war's urgency, and was sent to the Todd Shipyards in Brooklyn for thorough refitting. During the alterations, she was given new oil-fired turbines and a single, smaller funnel, before being able to return to military work in 1943 for the US Army.

When the war finished, her future seemed bleak. Her age almost prevented any further service although there were any number of European firms who might have bought or chartered her for immigrant and displaced persons' sailings. The possibilities of any kind of revival became less likely when she was badly damaged by fire in New York in March 1947. Temporarily patched, the *George Washington* was removed to Baltimore and laid up, only to be swept by a second, more serious fire which erupted on the pier and spread. The end came on January 17 1951. What remained of the wrecked hull was simply scrapped.

Gross tonnage: 25,570 (1909), 23,788 (1920)
Length: 723 feet
Width: 72 feet
Machinery: Steam quadruple-expansion engines geared to twin screw
Speed: 18.5 knots
Capacity: 568 First, 433 Second, 452 Third, 1,226 Steerage (1909); 500 First, 377 Cabin, 614 Third, 1,432 Steerage (1920)
Built: A G Vulcan, Stettin, Germany, 1909
Demise: Destroyed by fire and then scrapped in Baltimore, Maryland, 1951

Above right 'The Big George' *sailing from Hoboken as a troop ship under American colours. Across the Hudson in Manhattan are the funnels of Cunard's* Aquitania.
Right *The First-Class writing room of the* George Washington. *Note the unusual lampshades.*

Left *On a rare occasion, the liner was dry-docked at the Philadelphia Navy Yard—July 1929.*

Below *The* George Washington *as seen during the 1920s in United States Lines colouring.*

Right *Fire trucks attempted to combat a blaze aboard the* George Washington *in March 1947 while she was docked at the Jersey City Army Pier in New York harbour.*

Below right *An Army Signal Corps photo dating from December 1943, showing the ship with a single, smaller stack.*

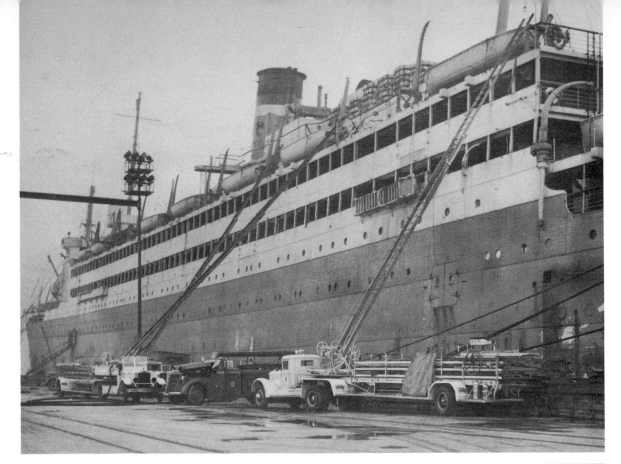

George Washington

Olympic

The White Star Line was in its greatest period in that first decade of the twentieth century. Although it had come under the control of Mr J Pierpont Morgan's International Mercantile Marine—the IMM, for short—it was recongised as the senior firm in that consortium and its ships were allowed to fly the British flag despite the American ownership. The White Star policy was to continue its forefront position among transatlantic firms and especially in its continued rivalry with the Cunard Line, but they did not have any ambitions towards capturing speed records. The emphasis was threefold, alternately: great size, luxurious accommodation, and moderate speed. Consequently, when White Star was challenged by the blazing success of Cunard's *Lusitania* and *Mauretania* of 1907, plans were drawn to create a trio of liners (three were needed to maintain weekly service between New York and Southampton) that would far outshine the Cunard pair both in size and luxury. There was absolutely no ambition towards gaining the Blue Riband from the *Mauretania*.

The trio were drawn up as massive 45,000-tonners plus, against the 31,000 of the Cunarders. The prestige and publicity of having the world's largest was invaluable as calculated by the White Star directors. Across the North Sea the Hamburg America Line was having similar thoughts, but to the theme of a trio between 50–60,000 tons. At best, the White Star liners would be the largest only for brief periods. The plans continued, however.

The original scheme was to name the trio *Gigantic, Titanic,* and *Olympic.* Building orders were given to one of the world's most masterful ocean liner builders of the day, Harland & Wolff in Belfast. However, somehow in the early translation of details, the original third name of *Olympic* was reassigned to the first ship. She was launched on October 20 1910 amidst tremendous excitement, while the guests who attended the ceremony could gaze aross to the next building slipway and see the early steel frame of the second of the sisters, the *Titanic.*

Befitting the largest liner in the world, the London and New York offices of White Star worked hard to create substantial enthusiasm both from the shipping community and from the travelling public. Particular attention was given to the outstanding level of luxury that would be found in the new liner. Descriptions included the Arabian indoor swimming pool (the first on a transatlantic liner) complete with bronze lamps and an ornate marble drinking fountain. The First Class cabins were decorated in eleven different styles of decor and the lush greenery in the Palm Court would remind passengers more of a land-side club than a sea-going public room. There were 1,054 berths in First Class (an incredibly high figure compared to most other Atlantic queens) and a further 510 in Second Class, but White Star realised that a goodly source of the liner's profits would come

from immigrants seeking passage to America. The 1,020 Third Class berths were often booked to capacity on the westbound crossings. Of the liner's four towering stacks, only three actually dispensed smoke and exhausts; the fourth was a ventilator and also contributed to the vessel's overall grandeur. Immigrants were very often impressed by the number of funnels on a liner and customarily sought the ship with the highest number for the 'voyage of their lifetime'.

White Star's greatest day came on May 31 1911. A large contingent of guests arrived at the Belfast yards for the noon-time launching of the *Titanic*, an amazing sight in itself. Then, in the afternoon, they boarded the brand new *Olympic* and sailed overnight to Southampton. The impression on these guests and visiting press was tremendously effective.

The *Olympic* left Southampton on her maiden voyage to New York on June 14 1911. As planned, she was hailed as the world's largest liner—45,324 gross tons and 882 feet long overall. The record went to the *Titanic* a year or so later and then to Germany's *Imperator* at 52,000 tons and 919 feet in 1913. However, tragedy was to mark the remaining years of the White Star fleet.

The *Olympic* was seriously damaged off Southampton on September 20, after colliding with the cruiser HMS *Hawke*. Six months later, in April 1912, the grotesque disaster of the *Titanic* took place. The *Olympic*—as direct sister to the ill-fated ship—was given an extended refit in the winter of 1912–13 in Belfast. Additional safety measures were installed and included the strengthening of the bulkheads and extra lifeboats that would more than comfortably take her more than 2,100 passengers and 860 crew members. At the same time, her accommodation was rearranged to 735 First Class, 675 Second and 1,030 Third, and the tonnage was reregistered at 46,439. Similar methods of safety were installed aboard the third of the original pair, the *Britannic* (the name *Gigantic* seemed an unwise choice on the heels of the sinking of the *Titanic*), which was then still being built. The *Britannic* eventually brought more tragedy to the White Star firm. At 48,000 tons and the biggest of the planned trio, she was commissioned as a troop ship in the fall of 1915, only to be sunk by a German underwater mine in the Aegean a year later.

During World War 1, the *Olympic* was for a time 'dazzle-painted' for camouflage at sea while trooping. An heroic episode took place in October 1914, when she attempted to tow the mine-damaged battleship HMS *Audacious* in the Irish Sea. In the end, the warship was too badly injured. Her survivors were transferred to the *Olympic*, the towlines were cut and the military vessel allowed to sink. On May 12 1918 the liner was attacked by enemy U-Boat 103. Miraculously, the incident was foiled and the *Olympic* managed to ram and sink the sub with the loss of all but one of its crew.

Once back in Belfast in August 1919, the post-war refit was a perfect opportunity to convert the liner from coal to oil-burning. The berthing again underwent some changes, this time in the ratio 750: 500: 1,150, and she was back on the Atlantic run in July of the following year. Eventually, her running-mates became the *Majestic* (the world's largest until the *Normandie* in 1935) and the somewhat more compact 34,000-ton *Homeric*. These ships were both prizes of war, seized by Britain as part of the dismemberment of the German passenger ship fleet.

The *Olympic* retained considerable popularity and was often sought by the Hollywood set for their annual travels to and from England and Europe. Her accommodation was twice changed during these years: first in 1928 to 675 First, 561 Second, and 819 Third, and then in 1930, to 618, 447, and 382.

The profit-making days began to disappear with the onset of the Great Depression. White Star was particularly hard hit and its liners were often sailing a third full. The *Olympic* and some of her fleet-mates were despatched on cruises, even one-day Bank Holiday trips out of Southampton. The crew were reduced, the accommodation lacked its customary lustre, and, more seriously, it was reported that only one side of the ship was being painted and looked after—the side that the passengers would see on arrival or departure.

The financially ailing White Star Line was merged with its one-time arch-rival, the more secure Cunard Company, in February 1934. After serious evaluation, the *Olympic*—among others—was placed on the disposal list, but not without one more chance at some headlines: on May 16, she rammed and sank the Nantucket Lightship outside New York harbour in thick fog; seven of the ship's crew drowned.

The *Olympic* was decommissioned and laid up in

Southampton in April 1935, and took her place alongside another unwanted peer, the former speed-breaker, *Mauretania*. Rumours of the day included one that the Italian government wanted to buy the *Olympic* for use as a troop ship in its East African campaigns. Nothing came to pass, as auctioneers and strippers climbed aboard and carted away some of her devalued fittings. The remaining hulk was sold to Metal Industries Ltd and arrived at Jarrow for scrapping in October. She was a welcome if sad sight to the hard-pressed scrap industry workers. The dismantling was obviously a slow process as she was towed to Inverkeithing two years later to complete the work. She was the last great reminder of the heyday of the White Star Line.

Gross tonnage: 45,324 (1911), 46,349 (1913)
Length overall: 882 feet
Width: 92 feet
Draft: 34 feet
Machinery: Steam triple-expansion engines geared to triple screw
Speed: 21 knots
Capacity: 1,054 First, 510 Second, 1,200 Third (1911); 735 First, 675 Second, 1,030 Third (1913); 750 First, 500 Second, 1,150 Third (1920); 675 First, 561 Second, 819 Third (1928); 618 First, 447 Second, 382 Third (1930)
Built: Harland & Wolff Limited, Belfast, Northern Ireland, 1911
Demise: Partially scrapped in Jarrow, 1935, completed in Inverkeithing, Scotland, 1937

The White Star four-stacker dwarfs three other IMM ships at the Chelsea piers, New York. On her far left is a Kroonland-*class liner, on her immediate left one of the* Adriatic *class.*

Above *The* Olympic *just after her launching.* **Below** *In dazzle paint during the Great War.*

Above *The* Olympic *laid up in Southampton with the* Mauretania, *in white.* **Below** *Getting up steam to leave Southampton for the scrapyard in October 1935.*

Titanic

It was pure coincidence that this chapter was Chapter 13. Coincidence and the *Titanic* have long been bedfellows. The long arm of coincidence is nowhere better illustrated than with this magnificent ship. In 1898 a novel called *Futility* was written by Morgan Robertson. It was one of four short novels published in the book, only 70 pages long. And yet, if Mr Robertson had been a prophet he could not have foretold the fate of the *Titanic* with greater precision. He began: 'She was the largest craft afloat . . . in her construction . . . were involved every science, profession and trade known . . . . On her bridge were officers, who, besides being the pick of the Royal Navy, had passed rigid examinations in all studies . . . .' Describing his mythical ship's watertight compartments he concluded that 'the steamship *Titan* was considered practically unsinkable.' Yes, his ship was named the *Titan*.

Writing before the *Oceanic* had been completed, Robertson said his ship was 800 feet long (*Titanic* was 882), that she boasted 70,000 tons displacement (*Titanic*'s displacement was 66,000 tons), had triple screws (so did *Titanic*), and could make 25 knots (*Titanic* could do this in spurts). The *Titan* carried as few lifeboats 'as would satisfy the laws'—only 24 (as did *Titanic* with only 16). He had her steaming at night in full steam in April, as was the *Titanic*. And she struck an iceberg and sank.

And then there was the extraordinary case of how the liner, *New York*, almost saved the *Titanic*. She was tied up near the big four-stacker as the *Titanic* sailed on her maiden departure. Suction from the new giantess pulled the older ship away from her pier and it looked as if a collision was imminent. But a little tug darted out and stopped the *New York* hitting the *Titanic*, thus saving the new liner and dooming her at the same time.

A good case can be made for the belief that the *Titanic* will go down in history as the most famous of all ocean liners. Perhaps 'best known' is a more fitting description, but certainly the *Titanic* has been written about more than any other steamship. The membership of the *Titanic* Historical Society in the United States is almost as large as the entire membership of the Steamship Historical Society of America. The passion for *Titanic* memorabilia never seems to be satisfied, is ever growing. The enthusiasm for finding the ship's sunken hull seems to grow each year. And there is even serious talk of attempts to salvage her 'treasures' and possibly even the ship herself. Is it all a case of morbid curiosity? Perhaps, but if it is only this then why is not the fate of the *Lancastria* or the *Wilhelm Gustloff* of equal fascination? Both went down with several times as many casualties. The fact remains that the *Titanic* and everything about her are of tremendous and very broad public interest. If and when she is actually found it will make one of that year's really great news stories.

Her brief life began on March 31 1909 when her keel was laid. Because she was the second of a three-ship building programme, White Star publicity people worked doubly hard to make her known. A 20-horse team delivered one of her anchors to the

shipyard. As shown in a marvellous picture in Walter Lord's illustrated edition of his *A Night to Remember*, children in their Sunday best walked alongside watching the procession. The anchor weighed 15½ tons. This and countless other statistics were sent around the world. She was launched on May 31 1911, and spent the next 11 months being fitted out as the most magnificent liner afloat. Like her sister, she only needed three stacks but a fourth was added for appearance's sake.

Her maiden voyage began on April 10 1912, from Southampton, where she had her close encounter with the old clipper-bowed *New York*—an omen of disaster, many would say later. She steamed across the Channel to pick up more mail and passengers at Cherbourg. She was too large to dock there and her people came out to her by tender. A last stop at Queenstown, Ireland, followed. Many emigrants boarded her there and a second bad omen occurred, as remembered by Lawrence Beesley, one of her most articulate survivors. A stoker, black with soot, climbed up inside the dummy funnel and was seen by many waving and grinning. An American lady aboard confided later in Beesley that she was sure this was a sign of very bad luck and the real reason why the ship had sunk.

The collision with the iceberg took place just before midnight on April 14. Six compartments were ripped open below the waterline. By 2.20 a.m. the liner had plunged beneath the waters of the Atlantic. There were 1,316 passengers aboard, of whom 825 died that night, and 885 in the crew, of whom 673 perished. The western world was shocked as by no other single event in modern history.

Gross tonnage: 46,329
Length overall: 882 feet
Width: 92 feet
Draft: 34 feet
Machinery: Steam triple-expansion engines geared to triple screw
Speed: 21 knots, plus
Capacity: 905 First, 564 Second, 1,134 Third
Built: Harland & Wolff Limited, Belfast, Northern Ireland, 1912
Demise: Struck an iceberg on April 14 1912 and sank the following morning

The great size of the Titanic *is clearly evident in this photograph, taken in 1911 just prior to launching.*

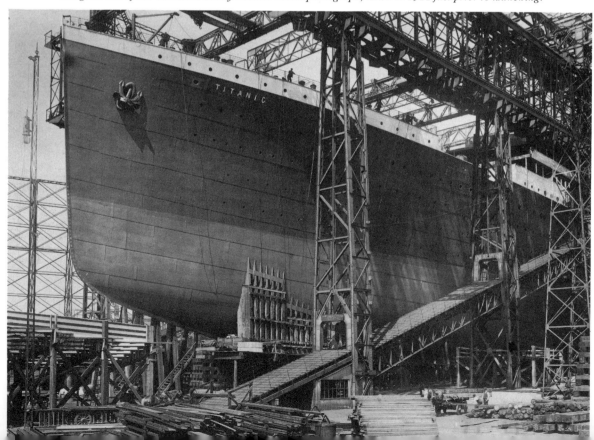

Above *On a very rare occasion when the two White Star giants were together, with the* Olympic *on the left. The* Titanic *is at her fitting out dock. The picture dates from early 1912 in Belfast.*

Below *The splendid proportions and graceful lines of the* Titanic *are apparent in this photo.*

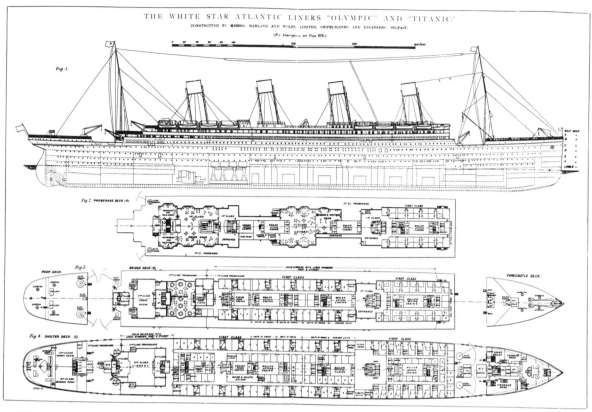

THE WHITE STAR ATLANTIC LINERS "OLYMPIC" AND "TITANIC."
CONSTRUCTED BY MESSRS. HARLAND AND WOLFF, LIMITED, SHIPBUILDERS AND ENGINEERS, BELFAST.
(For Description, see Page 676.)

Above *A side elevation and partial deck plan prepared by Harland and Wolff ship-builders.*

Left *The horrifying sight as the great liner lifts out of the freezing Atlantic and prepares to take the final plunge.*

Fifty Famous Liners

Imperator/Berengaria

The Germans—particularly the Hamburg America Line, guided by the genius and determination of its director Albert Ballin—were not to be outdone by their British contemporaries, namely Cunard and White Star, after that first decade of the new century. The keel was laid on June 18 1910, for what was called 'the colossus' of the Atlantic run. Even more astonishing, she was merely the first of an increasingly larger trio of liners that would surpass the imagination of the world in terms of size and luxury. However, like the rival White Star Line, the Germans were interested only in moderate speed and had no intention of racing with Cunard's *Mauretania*.

The new liner was to be called *Europa* and would be the flagship not only of the Hapag fleet but of the entire German merchant marine. However, as a result of the efforts of publicists in Hamburg, the interest of the Kaiser was aroused to such an extent that it was deemed even more fitting to name the ship *Imperator*. Her statistics were staggering: the rudder alone weighed 90 tons; there were 83 lifeboats plus 2 motor launches; the four-bladed propellers could make 185 revolutions per minute; there were two engine rooms, 69 and 95 feet long, and bunkers for 8,500 tons of coal. Her accommodation included a First Class saloon that comfortably seated 700 and was topped by a glass dome, and a series of cabins that included two sumptuously decorated 'Imperial' suites. Ballin, in his great wisdom, knew that transatlantic travel had grown substantially after the turn of the century, and that the demand for passenger spaces would continuously increase. He balanced his efforts between topflight luxury in First Class to improved standards in the Steerage quarters. Consequently, the *Imperator* was not only the world's biggest liner (at 919 feet in length and 52,000 tons), she could also transport the greatest number of passengers: 4,594 in all plus 1,180 crew members.

Worldwide attention was focused on Hamburg on May 23 1912, a little more than a month following the *Titanic* tragedy, when the Kaiser himself christened and launched the new liner. Some uneasy guests were reminded that a huge searchlight would be carried on the foremast, presumably to spot icebergs.

The *Imperator* was completed exactly one year later and left Cuxhaven via Southampton for New York on June 10 1913. Despite the gaiety of the occasion, the ship's lavishness had sent the Vulcan Shipyards of Hamburg into bankruptcy and her initial voyages were seriously marked by the fact that she was top heavy. She rolled notoriously, a fact that in Hapag's estimation could ruin her financially. The liners were furiously competitive at that time and their faults were often bandied about, with resulting fewer passengers. Therefore, in her first autumn refit, she had her monstrous three funnels (the third was a dummy) cut down by 9 feet to improve her balance. All upper deck panels and fittings were replaced by ones done in lighter materials, a bronze decorative eagle fitted on the bow was removed, and a substantial supply of cement was poured along her bottom. To some extent, the *Imperator*'s 'teething problems' were resolved.

Her commercial days were brief. When the Great War broke out, she was laid up in Hamburg, as it turned out for a period of over four years. Germany's masterpiece was suddenly neglected and was found to be in a decaying and rusted state by the invasion forces. She was fired up and used as the USS *Imperator* for trooping between May and August of

1919, but then ony to be laid up again in New York. A reprieve came when she was chartered to Cunard for their peace-time service, evidently as the most readily available replacement for the *Lusitania.* She was thereafter formally allocated to Britain and, with her intended third sister, the *Bismarck* (which was to become the *Majestic*), was sold to Cunard and White Star Lines jointly. As such, she sailed under her German name on Cunard's Liverpool/New York service, still in a somewhat austere state.

She was given the name *Berengaria* in April 1921 after an outright purchase by Cunard. She had already transferred her base to Southampton, and was noted as the first Cunarder to be named after a queen, in this case the wife of Richard the Lion Heart. Despite her German heritage, she was made flagship of the Cunard fleet, in preference to the smaller *Aquitania* (45,600 tons) or the record-breaker *Mauretania* (still the world's fastest liner).

Eventually, time was set aside for a six-month refit, beginning in October 1921, that would bring the ship more in line with the standards and desires of her new owners. She was converted from coal to oil-burning, and fitted with bunkers that could hold 6,500 tons of fuel, against her consumption of 700 tons per day on her Southampton/New York crossings. More cement was poured into her bowels to reduce rolling at sea and much of the original heavy marbles in First Class were removed and replaced with metal fittings. The passenger quarters were restyled to suit the 1921 American immigration quota regulations: 972 First Class, 630 Second, 606 Third, and 515 Tourist. The overhaul was a success in that on a crossing during the following year she achieved her best time: 23.79 knots.

The *Berengaria* was a respected member of Cunard's famous 'Big Three' (the others being *Aquitania* and *Mauretania*) that ran the weekly Atlantic service, which was particularly competitive with White Star's *Majestic, Olympic,* and *Homeric.* Her passenger rosters often included famous names and on one sailing she carried the Prince of Wales (later the Duke of Windsor).

When the Depression set in, the *Berengaria* was rather sadly affected. Her transatlantic crossings were more often less than half full, resulting in her frequently being detoured to inexpensive cruising—south to Bermuda and the Caribbean, and on weekend jaunts along the Atlantic coastline to

The gigantic Imperator *at dock in Cuxhaven after her funnels have been reduced in height to improve stability.*

Halifax, Nova Scotia. Her clientele had changed considerably and one of her former patrons referred to her as the 'Bargain-area'. She was included in the Cunard-White Star merger of 1934, but was fortunately not in the rather large disposal list created following that union of firms.

In September 1935, she established something of a unique record. In Southampton, she had a turn-around time of a mere 13¼ hours in which more than 1,000 passengers and their baggage were handled, over 4,000 bags of mail processed, 7,000 tons of fuel oil pumped into her bunkers, 1,000,000 gallons of fresh water put into the tanks, and 30 tons of ships stores taken aboard.

The Cunard plan was to keep the *Berengaria* in service through 1940 and then to replace her with the new *Queen Elizabeth*. In the interim, she was used to balance the service between the new flagship *Queen Mary* and the old *Aquitania*, but somehow her age created a serious dilemma: fires resulting from outmoded wiring systems. In 1936, there was a blaze along the Southampton docks, only to be followed by one far more serious in New York two years later. Inspection by American authorities caused her passenger certificate to be revoked and, despite protests by Cunard officials, she was forced to return to England without passengers. The situation became even more obvious when, in Southampton, a third damaging fire erupted. Cunard faced the fact that the *Berengaria* would not survive until 1940.

The great liner was offered for sale in October 1938, but had no serious bidders, especially since the major overhaul that she required would easily cost several millions in a period when passenger traffic was still in a slump. Consequently, she was bought by scrappers and taken to Jarrow, where she was cut down to the waterline. In retrospect, she might have been saved, even after being laid up for a time, for that costly refit might have been justified had she been used as a trooper after September 1939.

Strangely, however, the *Berengaria* did survive another Great War if only in a partial state. Her double bottom survived until 1946, when it was finally cut in two and towed to Rosyth for final demolition. Of the three early German giants, she survived the longest.

Gross tonnage: 52,117 (1913), 52,226 (1922)
Length overall: 919 feet
Width: 98 feet
Draft: 35 feet
Machinery: Steam turbines geared to quadruple screw
Speed: 23 knots
Capacity: 908 First, 972 Second, 942 Third, 1,772 Steerage (1913); 972 First, 630 Second, 606 Third, 515 Tourist (1922)
Built: Vulcan Werke, Hamburg, Germany, 1913
Demise: Scrapped in Jarrow, 1939; completely dismantled in Rosyth in 1946

Above right *The sumptuous indoor pool had a second storey visitor's gallery.*
Right *The ornate potted-palm luxury of the First-Class Winter Garden.*
Below *A cut-away drawing shows the enormous proportions of the ship.*

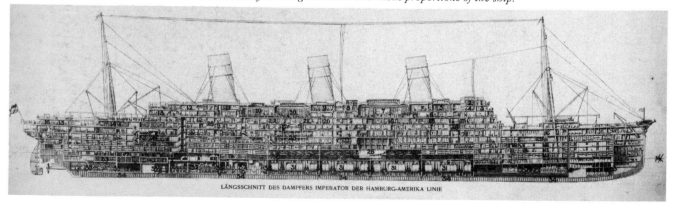

LÄNGSSCHNITT DES DAMPFERS IMPERATOR DER HAMBURG-AMERIKA LINIE

Fifty Famous Liners

Wintergarten I. Klasse.
Winter garden first Cabin.

Imperator/Berengaria

Left *Following a fire, the* Imperator *was partially flooded and listed toward her Hoboken pier. Note the decorative eagle on her bow.*

Right *Renamed the* Berengaria, *she is about to dock at New York's Pier 54. In the background (left to right) are the* Conte di Savoia, *the* Ile de France, *the* Lancastria, *the* Transylvania *and the* Majestic.

Left *In this view from the very top of the biggest floating crane in Southampton, workers continue their overhaul well into the night aboard the* Berengaria.

Fifty Famous Liners

Imperator/Berengaria

France (1912)

When the keel was laid, on April 20 1909, for the new flagship of the French merchant marine, it represented a bold step forward. The new vessel was to be more than twice the size of any previous French passenger liner. It had been intended to call her *La Picardie*, but at the time of launching (September 20 1910), the name *France* seemed far more appropriate. Considerable attention focused on the ship, even though the British and Germans were building or contemplating far bigger ships. Her decorations promised to make her one of the most luxurious on the North Atlantic and, not only was she France's first turbine-driven passenger liner but also one which featured an auxiliary engine room abaft of the main engine room. With four four-bladed propellers that were nearly 13 feet in diameter each, she was intended to do as much as 25 knots at sea (this against, for example, the proposed 21 knots for the much larger *Titanic*, then being built in Belfast). The coal bunkers had a capacity of 5,045 tons, allowing for a daily consumption of 680–720 tons.

The *France* departed from Le Havre on her maiden voyage to New York on April 20 1912, a mere six days following the *Titanic* disaster. Once in Manhattan, she put into a berth immediately adjacent to the one that would have been used by the ill-fated White Star liner. The French Line was more than grateful that the original design of their flagship included a sufficient number of lifeboats.

The *France* settled in on the Atlantic circuit quite quickly, and was highlighted not only by her superb decor but by her magnificent cuisine. Her First Class accommodation was favoured by the transatlantic social set, those millionaires and social aristocrats who ferried to and from Europe and America, often on more than an annual basis. Below decks, her westbound crossings were often booked by as many as 800 in Steerage Class. Although her propellers were changed in 1913 to improve her speed, overall she was considered an outstandingly successful ship and prompted the French Line to sign a mail contract with the French government for at least four larger liners (the 34,000-ton, three-funnel *Paris* was launched as the first of these in 1916).

When World War 1 erupted in the summer of 1914, the *France* was temporarily laid up in Brest for safety. However, her value as a troop ship was quickly realised and she was transferred to the French government, renamed *France IV*, and despatched to the Dardanelles. A year or so later, in November 1915, she was dry-docked at Toulon for conversion to a hospital ship, complete with full white colouring, a bold red stripe, and vivid Red Cross markings. She handled thousands of wounded servicemen over the next two years, all with the good fortune of being free of attack. In 1917, she had another overhaul at Toulon, this time for conversion back to a troop ship. A year later, she began the task of returning American military personnel. A form of more regular Atlantic service began in January 1919, again carrying soldiers mostly, between Brest and New York. Sailings were switched to Le Havre in August of that same year, formally re-establishing the French Line service.

The *France*'s fine reputation was reaffirmed during the 1920s, and included the fond dubbing of the liner as the 'Chateau of the Atlantic'. Time was finally alloted between October 1923 and May 1924 for a very extensive refit at the Penhoët Shipyards of

St Nazaire where she was converted to oil fuel, in keeping with all other major Atlantic ships. The accommodation was improved and modernised, and rearranged in view of the then recent American immigration restrictions. The new berthing system cut the Steerage capacity from 800 to 152.

Some misfortune struck on June 16 1928, when she hit a wreck in the Hudson River, New York, seriously damaging her propellers. Repairs were quickly made, but her future was facing stronger and more serious consideration by the directors of the French Line. She was now third in rank within the fleet, being surpassed by the *Paris* and the extremely modern *Ile de France*. Consequently, the *France* being the oldest both in style and appearance, she was shifted to periodic cruising, to the West Indies, the Norwegian fjords, and throughout the Mediterranean.

Once the Great Depression set in, her cruising work became more of an essential alternative to the declining transatlantic trade. She proved popular, lazily travelling from port to port with two or three hundred millionaires aboard. Her reputation as a notorious roller at sea seemed hardly to matter. Her kitchens were still excellent and the accommodation handsome, even if a bit dated by the sleek standards of the early 1930s.

She was damaged in a collision with the Italian freighter, *Carmia*, off the Ambrose Lightship, New York, on July 7 1931. After repairs, she was back at work in the cruise trades. However, when even more severe effects of the Depression were felt, the *France* became the first major French Line casualty. She completed her final sailing in August 1932, and was thereafter laid up in Le Havre, presumably only until 'better times'. Even in solitude, however, she was not immune to the more serious hazards that can befall an ocean liner. During 1933 she suffered fire damage that further jeopardised her chances of eventually returning to service. In December 1934 she was sold for scrap to breakers in Dunkirk. She left Le Havre under tow on April 15 1935, just weeks short of the maiden sailing of a newer French flagship, the 79,000-ton *Normandie*.

Gross tonnage: 23,666
Length overall: 713 feet
Width: 75 feet
Machinery: Steam turbines geared to quadruple screw
Speed: 24 knots
Capacity: 534 First, 442 Second, 250 Third, 800 Steerage (1912); 517 First, 444 Second, 510 Third, 152 Steerage (1924)
Built: Penhoët Shipyards, St Nazaire, France, 1912
Demise: Scrapped in Dunkirk, 1935

Maiden arrival of the four-stacker France *in New York April 26 1912.*

France (1912)

Above *The* France *in her war paint.* **Below** *A cross-Hudson ferry is seen at her stern as the* France *leaves New York.*

Aquitania

Many thought she was the most handsome of the four-stackers, a point well reinforced when she was fondly nicknamed the 'Ship Beautiful'. To this day, her wonderful sounding name (after the ancient Roman province in south-west France) immediately conveys the image of a mighty ocean liner, one of the illustrious 'floating palaces' of the era immediately before the Great War. The *Aquitania* was long and slender, with four well-balanced funnels (all of which worked, unlike many of the other three and four-stacked ships) and a pleasing counter stern.

She was ordered from John Brown & Company of Clydebank (the same yard that would later build the *Queen Mary* and the *Queen Elizabeth*) in December 1910, with her designs under strict Admiralty supervision. Although the war was still over three years off, the idea that such a major liner could be used as an armed merchant cruiser had high marks at Admiralty House. Otherwise, the plans called for her to be a well-decorated third partner to the speedy *Mauretania* and *Lusitania.* There was no intention that the new liner should compete for the Atlantic Blue Riband.

She was launched on April 21 1913 and left the Clyde a year later, in May, for three days of trials in which she reached 24 knots (a full knot more than expected). She left Liverpool on May 30, on her maiden crossing to New York, but her new commercial life was brief. In August, the *Aquitania* was requisitioned by the government for use as an armed merchant cruiser but, after a serious collision, it was decided that large ships were far too risky in such a role and that they were better suited to trooping and hospital work with military escorts. Consequently, in the spring of 1915, she was sent on troop voyages to the Dardanelles, and then converted to a hospital ship. In 1916, she was again trooping, and was laid up for most of 1917. A year later there were several more military sailings. She opened a Cunard 'austerity service' in June 1919, running between Southampton (Liverpool had been replaced as the 'big ship' terminal) and New York.

The return to her intended splendour did not begin until December 1919, when she docked at the Armstrong Whitworth yards in Newcastle for her major post-war conversion. Oil-fired equipment replaced the original coal, and all the original furnishings and objets d'art were brought out of storage and installed. The First-Class restaurant was done in Louis XVI style, giving the appearance more of a room in a chateau than in a passenger liner. The Jacobean smoking room was copied from a part of Greenwich Hospital, and the Palladian lounge had its own columns and rose two decks in height. Unquestionably, she was one of the best decorated of the Atlantic liners, even though the older style would later contrast sharply with the simplicity of ships like the *Ile de France* and the *Normandie.* Sadly, just as the *Aquitania* was completing her major refit, an engine-room explosion at the shipyard killed one of her crew.

When she returned to regular service in August 1920, she settled down to become the most popular liner on the Atlantic for the next two decades. Not only was she a favourite with the Hollywood set (silent film kings and queens were photographed at her rails on a weekly basis), but there came also royalty, government officials, inventors, great athletes, and more. In addition, she seemed to have particular appeal to those travellers who did not

favour one particular ship. She sailed in weekly tandem with the larger *Berengaria*, then Cunard's flagship, and the Atlantic speed champion, *Mauretania*.

Another major overhaul came in 1926, when her accommodation was adjusted: from 618 to 610 in First Class, from 614 to 950 in Second, and from 1,998 in Third to 640 in Tourist Class.

She was sent periodically on cruises, particularly to the Mediterranean, during the early years of the Depression, and had at least one troop voyage to Palestine. Even in the 1930s, she was performing well, still averaging 23 knots, and after new propellers were fitted in 1936 she often reached 24 knots. She was refitted again, during 1933, a process which employed 1,000 workers for three months. One new addition was a sound cinema. She went aground twice during these years: once at Calshot Spit but was refloated in 2½ hours, and then off Southampton on returning from a Mediterranean cruise during a 60 mph gale that kept her in place for 26 hours before being freed by 11 tugs.

After 1936, she was paired with the brand new *Queen Mary*, at least until 1940 when she could be replaced by the *Queen Elizabeth*. The Cunard plan was to have her scrapped at that point. The plans quickly changed when war broke out again in that fateful late summer of 1939. The initial plan was to have the *Aquitania* converted to an armed merchant cruiser, despite her total failure as such in 1914. Then the order was changed and she was outfitted as a trooper with space to carry 7,724 persons.

Her second World War was no less distinguished than her first. In eight years of further military work,

she sailed over 500,000 miles and carried 300,000 servicemen, to spots as distant as Australia, the South Pacific, and the Indian Ocean. Her record was heroic and she was the only one of the pre-1914 giants to survive such duty.

The *Aquitania* carried war brides in 1946–8 and was then returned to Cunard, hastily refitted and repainted in the company colours, and pushed out on an 'austerity service' between Southampton and Halifax carrying immigrants, displaced persons, and the last remaining troops. There were 12 such voyages in 1948, and a further 13 during 1949. She was never restored to her magnificent commercial self. One suspects that she might have continued for a few years longer but then mechanical and structural problems began to appear. She was not given a new operating certificate beyond her 1949 schedules. So, on December 1 of that same year, she reached Southampton at the end of her 443rd voyage, after 35 years of service and 3,000,000 steaming miles. She also marked the end of an era as the last of the four-stackers. She reached Faslane on February 21 1950 and was promptly broken up by BISCO Ltd.

Gross tonnage: 45,647
Length overall: 901 feet
Width: 97 feet
Machinery: Steam turbines geared to quadruple screw
Speed: 23 knots
Capacity: 618 First, 614 Second, 1,998 Third (1914); 610 First, 950 Second, 640 Tourist (1926)
Built: John Brown & Company Limited, Clydebank, Scotland, 1914
Demise: Scrapped in Faslane, Scotland, 1950

Right *The long, slender hull of the* Aquitania *at the Clydebank yards of John Brown in 1913. Perhaps the most successful of all great ships.*

Aquitania

U.S.A.T. "Aquitania"
9 CA-42-873-PSF

Above left *The 'Ship Beautiful' as seen in this view from the 1920s.*

Left *The liner outbound in Southampton waters in June 1932.*

Above *The great ship in war dress, docked in San Francisco, in 1942.*

Right *A poetic photo, taken through a pier opening in New York.*

Aquitania

Vaterland/Leviathan

She was intended to show her owner's sincerity in his efforts to stop World War 1. The *Vaterland* was Albert Ballin's 'money on the line' that he was genuinely convinced the rivalry between Great Britain and Germany could be contained and did not necessarily mean war. Ballin, who was the brilliant head of the Hamburg America Line, by far the largest passenger-ship line in the world in the early years of the twentieth century, had long been the leader of the German peace party. He put his 54,000-ton liner, the world's largest ship, into service in May 1914. He lost his ship, his company, and his life. The public should have a better understanding of Albert Ballin and his efforts for peace.

The fate of the three great Ballin liners built at this time was only one of the tragedies of the 'war to end all wars'. The Ballin dream of a weekly service by 50,000-ton liners was never fulfilled. His first, the *Imperator*, became Cunard's *Berengaria.* Then came the *Europa,* renamed *Vaterland* for political reasons. She would be renamed *Leviathan* by President Wilson and would fly the American flag for most of her life. Finally the *Bismarck*, completed under duress after the war, was run by White Star as their *Majestic.* Their stories parallel those of the White Star trio: *Olympic, Titanic,* and *Britannic.*

When war began in 1914 the *Vaterland* became 'interned' in New York. For three years she was the centre of German society who held large fund-raising parties on board for victims of the war back home. There was a strong pro-German sentiment in much of the United States. Many gala parties were given aboard the *Vaterland* by those who hoped America would go into the war on the side of Germany. But this all changed and the ship became a 'nest of spies' as war hysteria became rife. The great ship was seized the day America entered the war. She was rebuilt with great difficulty because no plans were available for her machinery or her vast inner areas. Her war service as the 'Levi-Nathan', or the 'Big Train', two of her best-known nicknames, was an outstanding chapter in America's war experience.

Her reconditioning after the war was a protracted affair but finally, on July 4 1923, she returned to peace-time passenger service. William Francis Gibbs, the noted naval architect who had rebuilt her, had used every measuring trick to make her original 54,000 gross tonnage turn into 59,956 tons. This led her operators to claim she was the largest ship in the world, much to the consternation of White Star, whose *Majestic* should have had this title. The French Line later did the same thing to permit the *Normandie* to seem larger than the *Queen Mary.* Eventually, to save money, the ship was remeasured and her low-American tonnage turned out to be only 48,943 gross. American tonnage rules exclude the superstructure, so ships measured by them are 20 to 25 per cent smaller gross than ships measured by British rules.

Mr Gibbs also attempted to make the *Leviathan* seem to be the world's fastest liner. He ran her 1923 trials with the help of the Gulf Stream. Although she set a world's speed record at that time, she never

Vaterland*'s ornate bow decoration.*

broke the transatlantic record and was regularly beaten by the *Mauretania.* For all his spirit, Mr Gibbs was given the unheard-of assignment for a naval architect of actually operating the rebuilt *Leviathan* on her first six crossings as an American liner. Despite all the exaggerated claims about size and speed, the *Leviathan* was without question the second largest and the second fastest on the Atlantic, and that meant the world. All these rivalries and the fame she had earned during the war gave credence to the claims that she was 'the world's greatest ship'. Throughout her less-than-twelve years of peace-time service she made news continually. Everything she did made headlines. Her passenger lists were studded with famous names. She was in fact the best-known ocean liner in the Western world.

The *Leviathan* operated with many handicaps. No American company had ever owned such a large ship. Attempts to sell her to a private company were defeated for politically motivated reasons and she was run by the government most of her life. America was suffering at this time through its experiment with 'total abstinance' under the Prohibition Amendment to the Constitution. This meant that alcohol could not be sold on board. Nevertheless, the *Leviathan* did remarkably well. She often carried more passengers than her closest rivals and her average lists ranked with the best. Many historians, in writing about this ship, remember only her final years when she, like many other big liners of that time, became a white elephant. She passed to private ownership just before the Depression of 1929 and her fate was sealed. She was laid up after five crossings in 1934 and sold for scrap three years later. She sailed to the boneyard in early 1938.

Gross tonnage: 54,282 (1914), 59,956 (1923)
Length overall: 950 feet
Width: 100 feet
Draft: 35 feet
Machinery: Steam turbines geared to quadruple screw
Speed: 23 knots (maximum 25 knots)
Capacity: 752 First, 535 Second, 850 Third, 1,772 Steerage (1914); 970 First, 542 Second, 944 Third, 935 Fourth (1923); 940 First, 666 Tourist, 1,402 Third (1931)
Built: Blohm & Voss Shipbuilders A/G, Hamburg, Germany, 1914
Demise: Scrapped in Rosyth, Scotland, 1938

Left *The First-Class Social Hall of the* Vaterland. *Notice the bust of the German Kaiser in the centre. It was later removed when the ship was seized by the USA and bought by a restaurant owner from Connecticut.*

Below left *First-Class dining saloon during her Hapag period.*

Above right *Steerage deck scene in 1914.*

Right Leviathan *outward bound in the Hudson in the mid-1920s.*

Stavangerfjord

Some ships manage to survive for many years and often, in doing so, tend to endear themselves to the public in an extraordinary way. Norwegian America Line's *Stavangerfjord*—with a lifetime that spanned 45 years—was one such ship.

The Norwegian America Line had just commissioned its first passenger steamers, the original *Bergensfjord* and *Kristianiafjord*, when thought was given to a third running-mate. World War 1 suddenly erupted and the plans were slightly delayed. However, orders were signed and on May 21 1917 the *Stavangerfjord* was launched from the yard of Cammell Laird & Company of Birkenhead, England. She was an improved and slightly larger version of the earlier sister ships and was regarded as the last stage in the Norwegian America building programme. Then, the plans went astray. The *Kristianiafjord* went aground near Cape Race on July 15 and became a total loss. Thereafter, the *Stavangerfjord* was looked upon more as a replacement than as a complement to the fleet.

She was finally completed at the end of April 1918. Transatlantic service was still in question, even though the Great War was nearing its end. As a precaution, she sailed from the ship-builders to the safety of New York where finishing touches were added and plans made for her eventual operations. Her maiden voyage took place in September and was quite unique for a European liner. Instead of a west-bound maiden crossing from her home port to New York, she did the reverse, reaching Oslo after having already been to the United States.

She was in demand from the start, establishing herself with the Norwegian travelling community in particular. Her accommodation was arranged for 88 in First Class, 318 in Second, and 820 immigrants in Third Class. She and the *Bergensfjord* steadily worked between Oslo and New York, with stopovers in Bergen, Kristiansand, Stavanger, Copenhagen, and Halifax (the latter for the disembarkation of Canadian-bound settlers). At the New York end, the pair differed from most other liners in that they docked along the Brooklyn waterfront, several miles south of Manhattan Island and in an area that developed a sizeable Norwegian population.

The *Stavangerfjord* occasionally supplemented her services with summer cruises to Scandinavia and the North Cape. Also, she was improved on occasion. In 1924, oil replaced coal for firing her turbines. During the winter of 1931–2, in Bremerhaven, she was fitted with new turbines entirely, which increased her service speed from 16 to 18 knots. The time was used also to upgrade her accommodation and the styling was revised to 147 Cabin Class, 207 Tourist Class, and 820 Third Class.

She was to some extent fortunate to be laid up in Oslo in December 1939: for the following five years, she remained permanently berthed as an accommodation centre for crews from ships of the German Navy. Her interiors were left untouched and it allowed her to sit out the Second World War in relative safety, just as she had done in the First. As a stroke of extremely good fortune, the retreating Nazi forces did not damage or destroy her. Consequently, following brief repairs, she was able to make the first post-war commercial crossing of the Atlantic in August 1945. She was in particularly high demand at this time as most other liners did not return to service until 1947–8. The berthing plans were rearranged for the third time in her life. They now read: 122 First Class, 222 Cabin Class and 335 Tourist (with the latter as a vast improvement over the original Third-Class immigrant quarters).

She worked single-handedly until the arrival, in November 1949, of the motorliner *Oslofjord*. She was looked upon as a sturdy, reliable ship with cosy,

handsome accommodation, and continued to prove herself attractive to Norwegians and Norwegian-Americans. Her passenger lists included sportsmen, students, diplomats, business executives and, on one occasion, Crown Princess Martha of Norway, occupying both of the First Class de luxe suites.

Very favourable press followed a near tragedy in December 1953. While in the North Atlantic during a gale, with a complement of passengers wanting to reach Norway in time for the Christmas holidays, she was damaged and lost her rudder. For a time, she wallowed and was totally adrift. Nearby, the company's freighter *Lyngenfjord* answered her emergency calls and attempted to put her under tow. The line snapped in the gale forces and left the *Stavangerfjord* to her own devices. In a most remarkable accomplishment, the liner was guided only through the use of her twin propellers. In the process, over 14,000 messages were sent between bridge and engine room. Gloriously, she reached her destinations in proper time, thanks to her crew and much to the joy of her passengers.

The new 18,000-ton *Bergensfjord* was delivered in the spring of 1956, and the then 38-year-old *Stavangerfjord* was rumoured to be due for retirement. The North-Atlantic passenger trade was at the time still dominated by the ship although under threat from the air. Encouraged by what seemed to be a continuing bright future for Atlantic liners and by the devoted following that she still maintained, the owners gave the *Stavangerfjord* yet another major refit during the autumn of 1956. This time her carrying capacity was specified as 90 First Class, 172 Cabin, and 413 Tourist. While the *Bergensfjord* and *Oslofjord* spent almost half the year in cruise service, the older ship—soon to be the 'Dowager of the Atlantic'—spent the entire 12 months in service between Norway and the States.

By 1963, the general transatlantic slump in passenger ship figures was well under way and the effect had finally reached the *Stavangerfjord*, then aged 45. Norwegian loyalists proposed that she become a maritime musuem, a permanently moored merchant-marine training ship and, of course, a floating hotel. None of the ideas materialised. The liner left New York with a fireboat and tug escort in early December, but with less festivity than expected out of respect to the mourning period still in effect for President John F Kennedy. When she reached Oslo

A 1963 menu cover—refined and handsome.

on the 14th, her record was outstanding: 2,800,000 miles, 770 Atlantic crossings, and 500,000 passengers.

She was sold to Hong Kong scrappers for $420,000, and arrived in the Far East on February 2. Ironically, her final voyage was the longest and farthest afield of her entire career.

Gross tonnage: 12,977 (1918), 13,156 (1945), 14,015 (1956)
Length overall: 553 feet
Draft: 27 feet
Machinery: Steam quadruple-expansion engines and turbines geared to twin screw
Speed: 16 knots (18 knots after 1931)
Capacity: 88 First, 318 Second, 820 Third (1918); 147 Cabin, 207 Tourist, 820 Third (1932); 122 First, 222 Cabin, 335 Tourist (1945); 90 First, 172 Cabin, 413 Tourist (1956)
Built: Cammell Laird & Company, Birkenhead, England, 1918
Demise: Scrapped in Hong Kong, 1964

Stavangerfjord *leaving her pier on the East River, New York, as she sails for Norway.*

Bismarck/Majestic

The *Majestic* was the world's largest liner for 13 years, beginning with her completion in March 1922. Only the first of the so-called 'thousand footers'—the French *Normandie*—finally outstepped her. She began life as the *Bismarck*, intended to be the third and largest of Albert Ballin's superb trio of German giants (*Imperator*, later Cunard's *Berengaria*, and *Vaterland*, which became the *Leviathan* for United States Lines, were the earlier sisters) that were designed to give the Hamburg America Line and, in fact, the entire German merchant marine a unique position on the high seas. When she was launched on June 20 1914, the naming ceremony was to have been performed by Countess Hanna von Bismarck, the grand-daughter of the famous Chancellor who had died 16 years before. However, the launching bottle did not smash as intended and the Kaiser, who was standing nearby, stepped forward and did the honours himself. Thereafter, the excitement sadly ceased as the war had begun and the liner was laid up and untouched throughout the next five years.

In 1919, the unfinished ship was the focal point of several rumours. One stated that the Germans would keep her in order to re-establish their passenger trade. Another mentioned that she would be given to the French as reparations. In actual fact, under the Treaty of Versailles, she was given to the British in compensation for the loss of the 48,000-ton *Britannic*, mined in 1916. However, to the Germans, she symbolised their war-time defeat as they had been relying on her for the future revival of their merchant fleet. It had been discovered that the Kaiser, the Crown Prince, and the entire German Imperial Family were planning to make an around-the-world 'victory cruise' in the *Bismarck*. When the war ended, the Kaiser was in exile and the liner far from complete.

The British were anxious to take delivery of the liner due to the pressing needs on the North Atlantic resulting from war-time losses in terms of tonnage. Some 1,200 German shipyard workers were assigned to the ship but not without great resentment and humiliation, particularly as they were under the supervision of the British Allied Command.

Construction was carried out at a sluggish pace, especially as a result of the shortages of steel and then as a consequence of a shipyard fire in October 1920. In February of the following year, the still unfinished liner was sold by the British government to the Cunard and White Star Lines, together with her near-sister *Imperator*. White Star eventually acquired the intended *Bismarck*, but not without some further complications. When she was finally completed in March 1922, representatives and crew from White Star arrived in Hamburg to find the name *Bismarck* painted on her hull and her funnels in Hapag colours. Her new British master found his stateroom being used as a storage closet, forcing her new owners to make some last minute alterations themselves. The 956-foot liner sailed to the Irish Sea for her first sea-trials (ironically eight years after launching) and was there formally renamed *Majestic*.

Considerable press attention was given to the new ship, specifically because she was the world's largest passenger liner at 56,551 gross tons. Thereafter, a continuing battle ensued for this distinction with her former sister, *Leviathan*. A great honour befell the *Majestic* in August 1922, when Their Majesties King George V and Queen Mary visited her during Cowes Week.

The *Majestic* worked in coordination with the

four-funnel *Olympic* and the smaller *Homeric* on the Southampton–New York express service for White Star. She quickly developed a great reputation and those who worked closely with her dubbed her affectionately the 'Magic Stick'. She operated at 23 knots service speed but on occasion, specifically in 1925, reached 25 knots and once, for several hours, recorded 27 knots.

When the Depression began, the *Majestic* was sent on occasional cruises, often from New York on weekend runs to Nova Scotia and on familiar 'voyages to nowhere', a thinly disguised scheme to lure Americans from the restrictions of Prohibition. However, these lean years were troubled ones for the White Star firm. Staff cutbacks resulted in reduced maintenance and upkeep on the liners themselves and the *Majestic* occasionally steamed into port scarred with rust. She passed into the control of the new Cunard-White Star combination in February 1934, and was quickly earmarked for disposal as the transatlantic trade had slumped from over 1 million passengers in 1930 to less than half that figure by 1935.

The *Majestic* was laid up in Southampton in February 1936, with little hope of any future commercial service. She was sold on May 15 to T W Ward Ltd for breaking up, surprisingly after only 14 years of service. However, just after she had been stripped of most exterior fittings and had had her funnels cut down for the intended passage under the Firth of Forth Bridge in Scotland where she was to be scrapped, the British Admiralty bought her

for use as a boys' training ship. She was freshly outfitted by the Thornycroft Shipyards of Southampton for use as a permanently moored school for 2,000 young cadets. She was renamed HMS *Caledonia* (despite an active Anchor Line passenger ship of the same name) and arrived at Rosyth, Scotland, on April 23 1937 to take up her new government duties.

When war developed, after September 1 1939, the *Caledonia* began to be converted for transport work, which would have seen her return to service. However, on September 29 fire broke out, seriously damaging the superstructure and resulted in her sinking in an upright position. She was salvaged by the following March but proved to be beyond any form of economic usefulness. T W Ward—the same buyers from 1936—scrapped her on the spot in Rosyth, and finished the task by towing her remains to Inverkeithing in July 1943. It was the end to what was by then the world's fourth largest liner.

Gross tonnage: 56,551
Length overall: 956 feet
Width: 100 feet
Draft: 35 feet
Machinery: Steam turbines geared to quadruple screw
Speed: 23.5 knots
Capacity: 750 First, 545 Second, 850 Third
Built: Blohm & Voss Shipbuilders A/G, Hamburg, Germany, 1914-22
Demise: Scrapped in Rosyth, Scotland, 1940; work completed in Inverkeithing, 1943

An Imperial Airways flying boat glides above the Majestic *in Southampton. Union Castle's* Carnarvon Castle *is docked in the background.*

Above *Her last arrival in Southampton as a Cunard-White Star liner in March 1936.*

Below *Leaving Southampton to become the naval training ship HMS* Caledonia *in Rosyth, Scotland. Note that her funnels and masts have been cut down and that most lifeboats are gone.*

Homeric

When the Hamburg America Line introduced the 52,000-ton *Imperator* in 1913, its arch-rival—the North German Lloyd of Bremen—responded with far less ambitious plans. Their intentions lay in two 34,000-ton sisters, both comfortable and economical but hardly record-breaking in terms of size and speed. They did, however, represent the Lloyd's largest liners to date, easily surpassing the 25,000-ton *George Washington* of 1909.

The new twin sisters were to have a simple yet attractive profile: two rather tall funnels balanced between a mast at each end (departing from the four masts used in the *George Washington* only four years before). The first of the pair was launched as *Columbus* on December 17 1913, at the Schichau Shipyards in Danzig. The sister ship occupied the adjoining building berth and was to be called *Hindenburg.* The outbreak of the Great War in the summer of the following year changed the plans completely. Although 80 per cent complete, work on the *Columbus* was halted and she sat out the next five years untouched. The *Hindenburg* had reached the point where her double bottom was finished, yet she too was ignored thereafter.

In 1919, fresh attention focused on the two ships but their futures were to be determined by the Treaty of Versailles. Consequently, as part of the large

reparations allotment to Great Britain, the *Columbus* was ceded to that country and would never see service for her original owners. However, her sister was not included in the reparations group and although work on her was not resumed until 1922, it was for her intended German owners. She entered service to New York in April 1924, as *Columbus* (the name *Hindenburg* having been discarded).

Construction on the original *Columbus* was slowly resumed in 1919, despite the shortages of materials and the prevailing discontent among the shipbuilding crews once it had been determined that she was to go to the British upon completion. A year or so later, in June 1920, she was purchased outright from the British government by the White Star Line, with the intention that she would join the company's 'Big Three' on transatlantic service, the others being the four-stack *Olympic* of 1911, and the *Majestic*, another ex-German liner that was being finished for the British with similar feelings of resentment.

White Star sent its own staff to Danzig to supervise the completion of the *Columbus* immediately after the sale was completed. One of the first steps was to give her a customary White Star name, using the 'ic' suffix. *Homeric* was decided on as an appropriate choice and was new to the company's earlier lists. As the construction proceeded, it is interesting to note that her coal-burning engines were not replaced by oil-fired ones, which were coming strongly into fashion at that very time, particularly among the larger Atlantic liners. The accommodation was, however, of the highest standard and was in keeping with the styles expected on White Star passenger ships. If *Homeric* was far outstripped by the size of the 56,000-ton *Majestic* and the 46,000-ton *Olympic*, she matched them well in terms of decor.

The *Homeric* first arrived at Southampton on January 21 1922 where she had some minor adjustments made and fittings installed, and then departed on her maiden voyage to New York on February 21. The third and last of the three-liner team, the *Majestic*, arrived by May of that same year and the White Star's weekly Atlantic service was finally under way. The trio operated in direct competition to Cunard's threesome: *Berengaria*, *Aquitania*, and *Mauretania.*

The *Majestic* had the added attraction of being the world's largest liner (until the *Normandie* appeared in 1935), and the *Olympic* sailed under the accolade of one of the great 'floating palaces' of the pre-war era, with the affectionate nickname of 'Old Reliable'. White Star sought a cachet for the *Homeric*, but was at a loss. Instead, the ship developed one of her own. By sheer accident of construction, style and balance, she emerged as one of the steadiest liners on the North Atlantic. There were no other anti-rolling devices at the time and this reputation attracted a loyal following of ocean travellers for the *Homeric*. She now had her unique position among the Atlantic queens.

The original coal-burning equipment was gutted and removed during an extensive overhaul that began at the Harland & Wolff yards of Belfast in October 1923. When she resumed sailing, in the following March, it was pleasantly noted that her service speed with the new oil-fired turbines had increased from 18 to 19.5 knots. Such reserves of more than a knot were often useful for delayed sailings and during bad-weather crossings.

Homeric—and in fact the entire White Star fleet—was seriously affected once the Depression had begun. Financial difficulties surfaced by 1930, and the number of passengers aboard the 'Big Three' dwindled continually, even in the normally peak summer months. Consequently, by June 1932, she was among the first of the large transatlantic ships to

be diverted to full-time cruising. The *Homeric* was no longer part of the great North-Atlantic liner fleet. She cruised from New York, but also on short runs from Southampton and Liverpool—with rates as astonishingly low as £1 per day—on trips to the Canaries, West Africa, and the Mediterranean.

When Cunard and White Star merged in February 1934, the *Homeric* was one of the first ships to be placed on the disposal list. At that very time the Depression was showing its worst effects and liners were particularly hard hit. She survived until September 1935 when, after her last cruise from Southampton, she was laid up off the Isle of Wight, awaiting her fate. Ocean-liner gossip hinted that her original German owners wanted to buy her, but nothing came to pass. By the next February, she had been sold to T W Ward for scrapping at Inverkeithing. Her untimely end might be one of the cruellest results of the Depression. She was scrapped only 22 years after launching and, even more surprising, she had seen only 13 years of actual service.

Gross tonnage: 34,351
Length overall: 774 feet
Width: 82 feet
Machinery: Steam triple-expansion engines geared to twin screw
Speed: 18 knots, 19.5 knots (after 1923)
Capacity: 529 First, 487 Second, 1,750 Third
Built: Schichau Shipyards, Danzig, Germany, 1913–22
Demise: Scrapped in Inverkeithing, Scotland, 1936

The *Homeric represented Cunard-White Star at King George V's Silver Jubilee Review in Spithead, July 16 1935* (Courtesy of F W Hawks).

Homeric

Above The Homeric *entering her Southampton dry dock for a winter overhaul.* **Below** *A seaplane landed alongside during this visit to New York.*

Fifty Famous Liners

Mongolia

One of the most extraordinary accomplishments has been the shipyard's skill in transforming the aged, unglamorous passenger ship into an ultramodern sea queen. Such improvements have prolonged the careers of many liners. P & O's *Mongolia* of 1923 was one such ship that, by her end, had sailed under four different flags for four different owners, had had five names, and had traded to ports throughout the world.

The *Mongolia* was launched from the Armstrong Whitworth yards of Newcastle on August 24 1922 and left London for her maiden voyage on the following May 11. She was designed for the overall England–Australia trade, with space for 230 First and 180 Second-Class passengers. She was built with sheer practicality in mind, especially as indicated by her simple 'no-nonsense' profile and rather sombre accommodation. On outward voyages she was filled with immigrants and with general traffic on the homebound sailings. Overall, her construction and entry into service passed relatively unnoticed except that she was P & O's first liner to be driven by steam turbines.

Her life was quite uneventful with the exception of a 1931 refit which converted her accommodation to 800 berths, all Tourist Class. Then, by 1938, P & O had built several newer liners, including the five 'Strath' ships. The *Mongolia* was superfluous and placed on long-term charter to the New Zealand Shipping Company, renamed *Rimutaka*, and assigned to the London–Panama–Wellington service. Apart from the war years, she remained on the 'NZ route' until 1950, by which time the company had received new tonnage in the form of the 21,000-ton sisters *Rangitane* and *Rangitoto*. The *Rimutaka* left

British registry for that of Panama and her new owners, Compañia de Navegación Incres. Again renamed, she began sailing, as *Europa*, between New York, Plymouth, and Antwerp, and offered 500 Tourist-Class spaces.

Little more than a year later, in the autumn of 1951, her owners had a change of mind. She was modernised for cruising and renamed *Nassau*. Her new mainstay consisted of weekly cruises between New York and Nassau, a run greatly encouraged by the Bahamian government who were pressing for tourist development. Furthermore, her year-round service to the Bahamas was the first of its kind. All other passenger ships traded there only on a seasonal basis. Periodically, the *Nassau*'s sailings were extended to include Puerto Rico, Cuba, Haiti and/or the Virgin Islands.

During the following decade, she had several 'glamorising' overhauls. Her interiors were fully air-conditioned and two outdoor pools added to a rather extensive lido area; the public rooms and cabins were improved and she was painted in a striking combination of white and blue. In 1954, she changed her flag for the Liberian one.

By the fall of 1961, strong competition forced the Incres Line to retire the 38-year-old ship. It seemed doubtful that further service was likely, but she did in fact go to a new group under the Mexican flag. An extensive refit followed at the Fairfield yard in Glasgow. Her owners—the Natumex Line (Naviera Turistica Mexicana)—had her renamed *Acapulco*

Mongolia

91

and sent her back to New York for a gala maiden voyage. This inaugural run was scheduled for Christmas 1961, to the Caribbean, through the Panama Canal, terminating at her new home port of Acapulco. Just before sailing, American authorities failed to pass the liner in a safety inspection, resulting in cancellation of the debut and she sailed to Mexico without passengers. On the Los Angeles to Mexico cruise run, her misfortunes continued as she failed to attract passengers and quickly became a financial burden. One slight reprieve came during the summer of 1962. She sailed to Seattle and was chartered for several months for use as a floating hotel, alongside the *Dominion Monarch*, another former British passenger ship. Together, the two filled the need for accommodation during the successful World's Fair of that year.

When the *Acapulco* returned to the cruise trades, her sailings were still poorly booked and all possi-

bilities were exploited, including business luncheons held while she was docked in Los Angeles. In the end she spent some time at anchor at the Mexican resort of Manzanillo, laid up and without purpose. In October 1964, she was towed slowly across the Pacific to Osaka, Japan, for scrapping. Her long career was over.

Gross tonnage: 16,385 (1923), 16,504 (1928), 16,596 (1931)
Length overall: 573 feet
Width: 70 feet
Draft: 30 feet
Machinery: Steam turbines geared to twin screw
Speed: 16 knots
Capacity: 230 First, 180 Second (1923); 800 Tourist (1931)
Built: Armstrong Whitworth Shipbuilders Limited, Newcastle, England, 1923
Demise: Scrapped in Osaka, Japan, 1965

An early photograph of the Mongolia *about to dock in Sydney.*

Fifty Famous Liners

RIMUTAKA - BR.
9-23-43 IN
U.S. COAST GUARD

Above Rimutaka *as photographed during World War 2 by the US coastguard.*

Below Nassau *inbound in New York in the early 1950s* (Courtesy of Moran Towing).

Above *The cruise ship* Nassau *in New York.* **Below** *At Pier 42, Hudson River* (Courtesy of Bill Rau).

Bottom *The ship's final period was as Mexico's first liner, the* Acapulco (Courtesy of Alex Duncan).

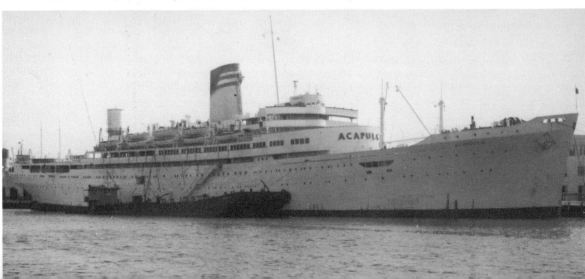

Albert Ballin/Hansa

Just before the Great War, in 1913, the Hamburg America Line—familiarly known as Hapag—had the largest merchant fleet in the world. There were 175 ships, with a combined tonnage of 1.3 million, and all headed by the 52,000-ton *Imperator*, then the world's biggest and most luxurious liner. The driving force behind the Hapag fleet was Albert Ballin, a maritime genius who was deeply nationalistic and felt that great size and astounding accommodation were the bywords of the future on the transatlantic run. His dreams included two further giants, the 54,000-ton *Vaterland* and the 56,000-ton *Bismarck*. Then the war changed all. In 1919, Hamburg America was left with a handful of coastal and harbour vessels. Its once glorious fleet was either lost in action or seized as reparations. Ballin himself was shattered and took his own life.

Slowly the firm began to emerge, but with new thoughts. The concept of ocean-liner supremacy was swept aside and replaced by one that emphasised medium size and economical operations. The Atlantic trade had changed substantially, particularly as a result of the then new American Quota System, which greatly regulated the flow of immigrants. The Steerage numbers had dropped from 1,000,000 in 1914, to a scant 150,000 by 1924 and the blueprints for the first new post-war Hapag liners were very much affected by this change.

The ideas centred about four ships, a pair each of similar design. The first sisters were of truly conservative type, having low, almost squat funnels and four masts, and presented a sharp 'no-nonsense' style. *Albert Ballin* was the name selected for the first ship. She was launched at the Hamburg yard of Blohm & Voss, the master German shipbuilders, on December 16 1922, and was ready for her first sailing on the following July 4.

She was registered at 20,815 gross tons, measured 627 feet overall, and had accommodation that was listed as 251 First, 340 Second, and 960 Third Class. With a service speed of 15.5 knots, which represented the extreme aspect of her economy, she was still able to travel between Hamburg and New York, with stops at Southampton and Cherbourg, in ten days. Her sister, the *Deutschland*, joined the service in mid-March 1924. The second pair, the *Hamburg* and the *New York*, which were of slightly different design and larger, at 21,500 tons, were added in 1926 and 1927 respectively.

Accommodation aboard the *Albert Ballin* was very comfortable, if not startlingly luxurious. The First-Class section, which occupied six decks, was quite smart and well-designed. Outdoors, there was a full-size tennis court and, for a time, an open-air bowling alley. There was a special grill room, which boasted a superb à-la-carte menu and stressed its exclusivity by requiring a reservation fee. Further along, there was a glass-enclosed promenade, a smoking room, writing room, library, ladies' parlour, social hall, and verandah café, the latter being filled with a vast display of green plants and shrubs. The ordinary dining room was accompanied by one especially for children. A gymnasium adjoined a tiled, indoor swimming pool, and for extra comfort there was an elevator, gift shop, and florist.

The First-Class cabins included four de luxe suites, each of which consisted of a foyer, sitting room, bedroom, baggage room, and full bath. Thirty special cabins had full-size bedrooms and bathrooms. The remaining staterooms were without private facilities and also lacked hot and cold running water.

The Second-Class quarters were quite comfortable, balanced by a variety of public rooms. Third Class was the most spartan, with blandly furnished public rooms and high density cabins. For all of their lives, the *Ballin* and her three running-mates—known as the 'Famous Four'—were very popular, with Germans emigrating to the United States and then, as German-Americans, travelling to and from the fatherland.

Possibly, one further aspect of the *Ballin*'s design added to her considerable popularity. She had the unusual feature of Foerster stability bulges that extended the full length of the ship just above the waterline. Together with hydrostatic valves, these bulges were claimed to have reduced rolling at sea to within five-sixteenths of normal. Additional help came from Frahm antiroll tanks, a system devised and used on several pre-World War 1 German liners. Consequently, the *Albert Ballin* and her sisters were said to be the steadiest liners on the North Atlantic.

Hamburg America designers constantly sought to

improve the *Ballin* and her sisters with the result that the ships underwent an astonishingly high number of alterations. In 1924–5, her original low funnels were heightened. The bridge was fitted with a glass enclosure in 1927. In 1930, she went back to her builders in Hamburg and was given new boilers that produced an increased service speed of 19.5 knots. The funnels were reduced in height and the bridge front again altered. More changes were made in 1934, in another visit to the Blohm & Voss yards. She was lengthened by the insertion of a new section forward, jumping from 627 to 677 feet. Her funnels were raised once more and the engines readjusted to make a service speed of 21.5 knots. Time was also given over to the accommodation, which was improved and revised to 204 First, 361 Tourist, and 400 Third Class. Also on this occasion misfortune struck. While being repositioned at the shipyard, she rammed and sank the North German Lloyd tug *Merkur.* Seven of the tugboat's crew were lost.

The *Albert Ballin* was the subject of an unpleasant dispute during the summer and early fall of 1935. The ever-growing Nazi Movement noted that the ship was named after a person who, though honourable and patriotic, was, nevertheless, Jewish. They pressed for a name change. Hamburg America resisted at first but then gave way on advice from the Berlin government. On October 1 the liner was renamed *Hansa.*

At the outbreak of war in the autumn of 1939, the ship was in Germany and remained there for the duration of the hostilities. She was used as a training and accommodation ship for the German Navy. Later, as the war neared its end, she attempted to dart into the Baltic from Gdynia with a full load of evacuees. She struck a mine but fortunately there was enough time for her desperate passengers to escape in the lifeboats. On March 6 1945 she quietly sank in shallow water off Warnemunde.

Four years later she was salvaged by the Soviet government and sent to Antwerp for repairs. The restoration was completed at Warnemunde, near the very site where she sank. It was painstakingly slow due to the post-war shortage of materials and further complicated by damages incurred during a serious fire in 1954.

Renamed *Sovetsky Sojus* (Soviet Union), she was commissioned as the largest passenger ship in the Soviet merchant marine in September 1955. Her tonnage had been raised to 23,009, and her appearance changed to two masts and one wide, tapered funnel. Little additional information was made available. She is based at Vladivostock in the Far East for 'government only' sailings to the Kamchatka Peninsular.

Just short of her fiftieth birthday, in 1971, she was given a very extensive overhaul at the Taikoo Dockyard in Hong Kong. This seems to have extended her life indefinitely. At the time of writing, in 1980, she ranks as the oldest major passenger ship still in service. Furthermore, it is quite amazing to note that her one-time 'Famous Four' running mate, *Hamburg*, which sank in 1945 as well, was raised in 1950 by the Soviets, commissioned seven years later as the whaling 'mother ship' *Yuri Dolgoruki* and was also listed in active service in 1980. The former *Albert Ballin* and her one-time fleet mate are great tributes to their builders.

Gross tonnage: 20,815 (1923), 20,931 (1930), 21,131 (1934)
Length overall: 627 feet (1923), 677 feet (1934)
Width: 72 feet
Machinery: Steam turbines geared to twin screw
Speed: 15.5 knots (1923), 19.5 knots (1930), 21.5 knots (1934)
Capacity: 251 First, 340 Second, 960 Third (1923); 204 First, 361 Tourist, 400 Third (1934)
Built: Blohm & Voss Shipbuilders A/G, Hamburg, Germany, 1923

A 1924 brochure describing the Deutschland *and* Albert Ballin.

Above left *With her original low smokestacks, painted all buff, the* Albert Ballin *was Hapag's first post-war liner* (Courtesy of the Vincent Messina Collection).

Left *Then a new stack colouring was adopted by Hapag* (Courtesy of the Vincent Messina Collection).

Above *The* Hansa *taking on fuel in New York.* **Below** *Still sailing, as the* Sovetsky Sojus *of USSR.*

Ile de France

The *Ile de France* was the first large liner to be designed and built after World War 1. At the time of her construction, the Paris offices of the French Line predicted that she would be the most magnificent liner on the North Atlantic. She was not intended to be the biggest or the fastest or in fact statistically notable in any way. Her appearance, while pleasant, was simply modelled after numerous other liners: three evenly slanted funnels with two large masts. But the French Line's excitement was churned by her interiors which were revolutionary. She was boldly and brazenly modern. Nothing like her had ever come from Europe's leading shipyards. She was an individual, not following the patterns set by other great ships but with a style of her own. She was a revolutionary, a trend-setter, and the inventor of the 'ocean liner' style of design. The architects and designers of the *Ile de France* did not copy even landside themes but created the first true floating luxury resort. In the words of the French Line President, Piaz, 'To live is not to copy.'

Her construction was underwritten by the French government as part of an agreement with the French Line (the Compagnie Générale Transatlantique) that dated from November 1912. The pact called for four passenger-mail liners that were to be built in five-year periods: the first in 1916, the second in 1921, the third by 1926, and the last for 1931. The 30,000-ton *Paris* was laid down in 1914 to fulfil the 1916 category, but World War 1 greatly disrupted her construction and she was not completed until June 1921. Therefore, the second liner was rescheduled for 1926.

On March 14 1926, at the Penhoët Shipyards of St Nazaire, amidst the presence of thousands of government and company officials, workers, their families and general spectators, this second ship was named *Ile de France* (Isle of France) and launched into the River Loire. Fourteen months later, on May 29, she left the shipbuilder's yard for her sea-trials, which resulted in a very pleasing 23.5 knots top speed. She returned for a brief survey in Brest and then sailed to Le Havre, her home port, where she docked on June 5. Once she was opened for public inspection, thousands of visitors—and particularly reporters from newspapers and magazines—were ecstatic in praise of the luxury and novelty displayed in the *Ile de France.*

The First-Class cabins, which numbered 390, were done in as many different styles and led one appraisal of the liner to assume that 'the *Ile* was more eclectic than modern.' Overall, she heralded the Art Deco age of the ocean greyhound through angular furniture, sweeping columns and panels, inventive lighting, and a prevailing sense of spaciousness. Each room seemed unique. The bar was claimed as the longest afloat, a feature which appealed immensely to the Americans, who were in the throes of Prohibition and who were to be her dominant clientele. The main restaurant, again said to be the largest of its kind going to sea in 1927, rose three decks in height and had a spectacular staircase as a main entrance. (The French Line's consideration for its female passengers, particularly in regard to dazzling entrances for dinner into a room filled to capacity, was always well appreciated. Grand duchesses, Hollywood film queens, and elegant dowagers more often rode the French liners than the more conservative British and German rivals.) The grand foyer was four decks high and the chapel was done in Gothic style with 14 pillars. There was a shooting gallery, a merry-go-round, and a well-equipped gymnasium.

Accommodation was arranged for 670 First Class passengers, 408 Cabin, and 508 Third. All cabins, including those for Third Class, had beds instead of bunks. First Class contained a large assortment of suites and de luxe cabins, and was acclaimed as offering the finest such selection at sea. By 1935, the *Ile de France* had carried more First-Class passengers than any other transatlantic liner.

On June 22 1927 she sailed from Le Havre, made a brief stop at Plymouth on the following day, and then proceeded to New York for a maiden welcome. Within her first decade, she was one of the Atlantic's most popular liners, averaging 795 passengers per crossing and this during the 'barren' years of the Depression. She was described as 'the cheeriest way to cross the North Atlantic', and was 'a bit of mainland France herself'.

In 1933, the *Ile*—which had suffered from serious vibrations—was sent back to her builder's yard in St

Nazaire and every piece of panelling was removed, padded, and then reinserted. At the time, just across the dockyard, the 79,000 ton *Normandie* was awaiting completion. Although still unnamed at the time, she was being described as the 'super *Ile de France*'. She was to be even more innovative, more revolutionary, and, in fact, to become one of the most outstanding ships of the century.

At the outbreak of war, in September 1939, the *Ile* was at New York's Pier 88, just opposite the great *Normandie*. The French Line had no desire to send the ship to her homeland, particularly in fear of enemy advances. The *Ile* was occupying an important Manhattan berth and was finally, under the care of ten tugs, towed to Staten Island, in the Lower Bay, to be laid up again. Her staff of 800 was reduced to 100. Months later, in March, she was put on loan to the British Admiralty and on May 1 was despatched to Europe and then Singapore with war materials. Once in the East, she was formally seized by the British after the fall of France.

She returned to New York in the autumn of 1941, and was handed over to Todd Shipyards Corporation for a 120-day conversion ready for trooping. Berths for 9,706 servicemen went in, plus new kitchen facilities, a total overhaul for the propulsion machinery, and the scrapping and replacement of the entire plumbing system. The *Ile* went back to trooping for the British government and served in the East again, with an Asiatic crew under P & O management. She sailed under dual flags: Britain and Free France.

Her first base port was Saigon and then switched to Bombay. Together with Cunard's *Mauretania* and the Dutch *Nieuw Amsterdam*, which were ships of similar dimensions and speeds, she worked the Cape Town-to-Suez shuttle. Then, by 1943, she was back on the North Atlantic, under Cunard management and with a European staff. She shuttled with assorted war-time passengers in company with the 30,400-ton *Pasteur*, which was built for France's Compagnie Sud-Atlantique in 1939.

The *Ile* was officially decommissioned by the British in September 1945. There was little time for repairs or a refit, and she was hurriedly sent on 'austerity' and repatriation voyages to Canada, New York, and even far-off Indochina. Finally, in the spring of 1947, she was handed back to the French Line and sent to the Penhoët yards for total rebuilding. The task took over two years. Her third and 'dummy' funnel came off and two more streamlined funnels were fitted in place of the other pair. Her berthing pattern was modernised to a more contemporary 541 First, 577 Cabin, and 227 Tourist-Class passengers. She left Le Havre on July 21 1949 on her first post-war commercial crossing to New York. It came as great relief to the 17,000-ton *De Grasse*, which from the war's end, had been acting single-handedly for the French. Both ships were joined in August 1950 by the 51,000-ton *Liberté*, totally restored as the national flagship from the pre-war German *Europa*.

The *Ile* made headline news on several occasions in the remaining years of her life. In July 1956, while outbound from New York, she rescued 753 survivors from the sinking Italian liner *Andrea Doria*. In October of the same year she was lashed by a violent Atlantic storm that flooded six passenger cabins and dented the superstructure. In February 1957, she went aground during a Caribbean cruise at Fort de France, Martinique. The damages were considerable. Her passengers were forced ashore and had to be flown home, while an ocean-going tug was summoned to tow the liner to the Newport News Shipyards in Virginia, the nearest facility capable of handling her in dry dock.

The *Ile* had her 31st birthday in 1958, the same year that aircraft overtook the passenger ship industry on the Atlantic. Her one-time high-society, First-Class trade had dwindled rapidly and the winter crossings had grown quite sparse. To complicate matters, the general problems of old age were setting in. Regretfully, her owners had to face the great ship's retirement and, in November, she sailed from New York for the last time. The decision sparked ideas for reprieve. One quarter wanted her for a museum, another for a hotel along the Riviera, and the Sheraton firm for a tourist centre on Martinique in the Caribbean. Many other schemes were more often based on nostalgia than practicality. The most ambitious suggested that her masts and superstructure be cut for bridge clearance so that she could be sailed along the Seine into the heart of Paris. The French Line was quite pleased when a Japanese scrap firm made an acceptable bid, thereby ensuring a quiet end in some far-away breaker's yard. The Paris office were fearful that some undignified end might befall their most famous post-war liner.

The Le Havre waterfront was crowded with well-wishers when the *Ile* departed for Osaka on February 26 1959. Under the command of a small Japanese crew, she hoisted the Japanese flag at sea and was dubbed the *Furansu (France) Maru*. Then, those fears of the Paris headquarters seemed bitterly and shockingly warranted. The scrap firm chartered the liner to a Hollywood film company, at the rate of $4,000 per day, for use as a floating prop in the production of *The Last Voyage*, a disaster-style movie based on the last sailing of a transpacific liner. The French went to court and succeeded in having the funnels repainted, at least partially, and barred the use of her famous name. Positioned off shore in the Inland Sea, the forward funnel was released and sent crashing into the deckhouse, the interiors made victim of explosive devices, and the watertight compartments partially flooded.

Eventually, the *Ile* was returned to Osaka and reduced to rubble. Her impact was considerable, her unique place in ocean liner history assured, and she is part of an immortal group that most historians think of as the most memorable twentieth-century liners: the *Mauretania,* the *Titanic*, the *Normandie*, the *Queen Mary*, and the *Ile de France*.

Gross tonnage: 43,153 (1927), 44,356 (1949)
Length overall: 791 feet
Width: 92 feet
Machinery: Steam turbines geared to quadruple screw
Speed: 24 knots
Capacity: 670 First, 408 Cabin, 508 Third (1927); 541 First, 577 Cabin, 277 Tourist (1949)
Built: Chantiers de l'Atlantique Shipyard, St Nazaire, France, 1927
Demise: Scrapped in Osaka, Japan, 1959

Fifty Famous Liners

The 'fabulous Ile' in her original design with three funnels, making a Coronation sailing' from New York to England in May 1937.

Left *The splendid First-Class restaurant. Notice the grand stairway entrance and the three-storey height. Even the chairs were of unique design.*

Above right *Outward bound for war, the Ile leaves Staten Island, NY, on her first military voyage in May 1940.*

Below right *Returning to New York for the first time after the war, in the summer of 1949.*

Left *The main lounge extended nearly the full width of the ship.*

Fifty Famous Liners

Ile de France

Cap Arcona

The Hamburg-South America Line was the foremost German passenger ship company on the very lucrative and competitive service to the east coast of South America. Not only was the trade supported by a vast number of immigrants, the new settlers to the Latin American continent, but by a substantial First-Class business of diplomats, traders, merchants, and Europeans off on a holiday voyage. Consequently, several other firms had sizeable interests: Britain's Royal Mail Lines was headed by the 22,000-ton sister ships *Alcantara* and *Asturias*, the Italians featured the 21,000-ton pair *Duilio* and *Giulio Cesare*, while the French were planning the 42,000-ton *L'Atlantique*, which would finally emerge in 1931. The Germans were not to be left out.

The *Cap Arcona* was launched on May 14 1927 at the Blohm & Voss Shipyards in Hamburg and was to be Hamburg-South America's biggest liner yet. Her design called for a rather relaxed profile of three red-and-white evenly slanted funnels, two high masts and the unusual feature of a large open-air tennis court just aft of the third stack. She was 19 months under construction and was designed with the deliberate intention of reminding the travelling public of the *Cap Polonio*, an earlier three-stacker completed in 1914, that was exceptionally popular. The *Cap Arcona* was to be, however, without any question, the new flagship. She utilised some earlier features but included some more contemporary and novel ideas, for instance: every First Class stateroom was outside and was fitted with private bathroom facilities; a restaurant located above the promenade deck had 20 windows overlooking the sea; a full gymnasium; a heatable salt-water swimming pool; and the previously mentioned outdoor tennis court.

Great excitement filled Hamburg harbour on November 19 1927 as she departed on her maiden sailing. Her special design, with a 20-knot service speed, allowed her to make the passage between her home port and Buenos Aires within 15 days. En route, she called at the Channel ports, Spain and Portugal, the Canaries, and then crossed the South Atlantic to Rio de Janeiro, Santos, Montevideo, and Buenos Aires. She was—to the joy of her owners—an instant success. Until the arrival of the French *L'Atlantique*, she was the 'queen of the South American run'.

The effects of the worldwide Depression of the 1930s seem to have had little effect on the *Cap Arcona*. Other company passenger ships were detoured, more often to cruising, to the Northlands, the Mediterranean, and the Canaries. Even her influential predecessor, the *Cap Polonio*, was briefly turned into an exhibition ship in Hamburg, then laid up and finally scrapped in Bremerhaven in 1935. Her lifespan of 21 years was shortened by the economic conditions of the time.

In the later 1930s the *Cap Arcona* flew the Nazi banner and, as a consequence, carried fewer non-

German passengers. Particular security was used, especially in overseas ports, aimed at those opposed to the rising Hitler regime. When war erupted, in September 1939, she was retained at her home port and temporarily laid up.

On November 29 1940 she began service as an accommodation ship for the German occupation forces in Gotenhafen, Gdynia, Poland. She seems to have been permanently moored there, repainted in war-time grey.

By early 1945, as the war began to regress for the Nazis, the *Cap Arcona*—among other former passenger liners—was selected for the evacuation of the eastern territories. In three voyages she carried 26,000 evacuees to the German-held western ports. In April 1945 she was loaded with over 5,000 prisoners from the Neuengamme concentration camp, while anchored in the Bay of Lubeck. With the crew and guards it was estimated that over 6,000 were aboard.

On May 3 she was sighted by British fighter planes, attacked with rockets and fire bombs, and burst into flames. On board, panic broke out and, as she was hideously overloaded, the *Cap Arcona* capsized. Some 5,000 perished—a figure made even more agonising by the fact that these same souls were a matter of days away from freedom. Grotesquely, the former liner lay on its side with a third of its width poking above the water. After the Armistice, she was cut up on the spot.

Gross tonnage: 27,560
Length overall: 676 feet
Width: 84 feet
Machinery: Steam turbines geared to twin screw
Speed: 20 knots
Capacity: 575 First, 275 Second, 465 Third
Built: Blohm & Voss Shipbuilders A/G, Hamburg, Germany, 1927
Demise: Destroyed and sunk during air attack on May 3 1945; later scrapped on the spot

The launch at Blohm and Voss's famous shipyard in Hamburg (All photos of *Cap Arcona* courtesy of Blohm and Voss).

Left *Another superior view of the* Cap Arcona, *the new liner in dry dock before her trials.*

Below *Still another beautiful Blohm and Voss photo—the maiden voyage arrival in Montevideo.*

Below right *The First-Class saloon and* (**right**) *the First-Class dining room.*

Fifty Famous Liners

Cap Arcona

Augustus

The Navigazione Generale Italiana of Genoa had introduced two smart-looking, well-decorated passenger ships—the *Duilio* and the *Giulio Cesare*—on the transatlantic trade to New York in 1922–3. Their success was immediate. Therefore, the company directors saw no alternative but to capitalise on the market situation. The First-Class trade was quite lucrative while Third Class for immigration created an even balance, despite the American quota system of 1921. The design theme therefore concentrated on larger, more extravagant ships.

A pair was ordered from Genoa's Ansaldo Shipyards in 1925. They were to be of very similar proportions but with one rather startling difference: one would have the customary steam-turbine drive, while the other would use a diesel system then just coming into practical application. The 17,900-ton Swedish liner *Gripsholm*, completed in November 1925, had used diesels with considerable success. A month later, on December 29, the 24,000-ton *Saturnia* of the rival Italian Cosulich Line was launched and was acclaimed for her use of diesel machinery. Consequently, the new NGI liner, at 32,600 tons, would be the largest motorliner yet built.

Her near-sister and intended running-mate, the *Roma*, was launched first, on February 26 1926. She was by far the biggest passenger liner yet to be built in Italy and was, of course, the largest ever to fly that country's flag. The *Augustus* had her launch and naming ceremony at the end of the year, on December 13. Her diesel engines attracted world-wide attention and encouraged similar systems in numerous other passenger vessels to follow. She was indeed the biggest motorship in the world. Also, since she was over 100 tons larger than the *Roma*, she had the added distinction of being Italy's largest

liner, and as such remained unchallenged until the arrival of the 51,000-ton *Rex* in 1932.

Both the *Roma* and *Augustus* had an ornate, richly done First Class, which included some opulent suites, sizeable public rooms done in grand Italian decor and attractive outdoor swimming pools and lido areas. Both ships were in marked contrast to the very modern *Ile de France*, completed at the same time and which used more severe Art Deco styles. The twin Italian liners did not claim to be modern in decoration, but were representative of the more traditional Italian and Mediterranean stylings. They catered to a more specialised trade, namely the Italians themselves and to some extent Italian-Americans. While liners like the *Ile de France* were introducing stateroom accommodation for Third-Class passengers, the *Roma* and *Augustus* continued with the 'open berth' arrangement common to large liners before World War 1. Third-Class passengers had a minimal amount of space (the greatest being allocated to First Class), were berthed in vast dormitory-type sections and, in return, were charged very low passage fares. The Mediterranean passenger trade, either to North or South America, was still quite different from the North European operations where the capacities of Steerage Classes were reduced and improved in new Third-Class spaces. In all, the *Roma* and *Augustus* were designed for their specific passenger market and were overall quite outstanding passenger liners.

The *Augustus* achieved a maximum speed of 20 knots during her trials in October 1927, and glorified her MAN-type diesels. A month later, although intended for the New York run, she left Genoa on her maiden voyage to Rio de Janeiro, Santos, Montevideo, and Buenos Aires. Late in the following summer, she finally crossed to the United

States, the service being between Naples, Genoa, Villefranche (for French Riviera traffic), Gibraltar, and New York.

In 1931, partially as a result of the Great Depression, the Mussolini government decided that the three most competitive Italian transatlantic passenger lines should merge under the single heading 'Italia' (the Italian Line). Consequently, the ships of NGI—including the *Roma* and *Augustus*, as the largest—, the Lloyd Sabaudo, and the Cosulich Line became one, sailing under a single houseflag and repainted, with funnels in the state colours—green, red, and white. The merger had additional ramifications: it would present a more unified and competitive force to the north European lines and would simplify the building of two giant superships, the 51,000-ton *Rex* for NGI and the 48,000-ton *Conte di Savoia* for Lloyd Sabaudo. In January 1932 over a dozen passenger ships passed into the ownership of the new Italian Line.

Once the *Rex* and *Conte di Savoia* were in service, by the end of 1932, the *Augustus* divided her time between the New York and east coast of South America runs. She also made cruises and for this purpose was repainted with a white hull.

In 1934, with a slackening of the trades due to world economic conditions, she was given her first major refit. The accommodation was restyled to 210 First Class, 604 Second Class, 454 Tourist Class, and 766 Third Class, the total capacity dropping from the original 2,210 to 2,034. With this reorganisation, her gross tonnage was reduced to 30,418, although she remained the largest motor-liner afloat.

The Italians began a serious review of their operations in 1939. The *Roma* and *Augustus* were briefly, then permanently, laid up, with the intention that they would need greater service speeds and therefore major machinery overhauls. The plan continued that despite the success of the diesels in the *Augustus*, she would be converted to steam-turbine propulsion. However, as war erupted, nothing came to pass. In 1940, the *Roma* was re-engined for an estimated service speed of 30 knots, this in compliance with the scheme to rebuild her as an aircraft carrier for the Italian Navy. She had been renamed *Aquila* and was nearly complete when she was seized by German forces in September 1943. Earlier in that same year, the *Augustus* was cut down to the hull and began a similar conversion for aircraft military duties. It was intended to rename her *Falco*, but the name *Sparviero* was selected finally. The conversions on both former liners ceased with the German occupation.

The former *Augustus* was sunk on September 25 1944 by the retreating German armies so as to block the harbour entrance in Genoa. Nearly two years passed before the wreck was raised. She was sold for scrap to Italian buyers on July 7 1947. The former *Roma* was deliberately sunk in 1945 and then finally broken up in La Spezia in 1951.

Gross tonnage: 32,650 (1927), 30,418 (1934)
Length overall: 711 feet
Width: 82 feet
Machinery: MAN-type diesels geared to quadruple screw
Speed: 19 knots
Capacity: 302 First, 504 Second, 1,404 Third (1927); 210 First, 604 Second 454 Tourist, 766 Third (1934)
Built: Ansaldo Shipyards, Genoa, Italy, 1927
Demise: Deliberately sunk on September 25 1944; later salvaged and then scrapped 1947

A drawing issued in early 1928.

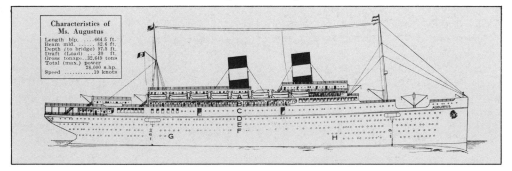

Above *The* Augustus *was Italy's largest liner from 1927 until 1932.* **Below** *She was repainted in the colours of the new Italian Line in 1932.*

Fifty Famous Liners

Kungsholm

After a sailing career of 35 years and under a trio of names, owners and flags, the cruise ship *Italia* steamed out of New York harbour in April 1964 for the last time, bound for a new career and her last role. Her cream-coloured hull and superstructure gave a gala appearance, one which is generally associated with a year-round cruise ship. She sported two, slanted, thin funnels and her two masts were noticeably shortened from their original height (so as to clear the bridges on the St Lawrence where the *Italia* had previously been employed). Her numerous lifeboats rested in their original quadrant davits. She was a grand-looking ship and one which had enjoyed a very full life.

The *Italia* was originally part of the illustrious Swedish American Line, which was affectionately known as the White Viking Fleet. She was commissioned in November 1928, as the *Kungsholm*, and was a slightly larger development of her running-mate *Gripsholm*, completed three years earlier and which became the German *Berlin*. Both ships enjoyed great popularity, both on the transatlantic run between Gothenburg, Copenhagen, and New York, and as single-class cruise ships, visiting ports around the world. These cruise services developed such renown that the Swedish American Line was sometimes more often remembered for that operation rather than for its North-Atlantic passenger trade. For the *Kungsholm*, cruising ranged from five-day sailings to Bermuda over the Thanksgiving holiday to a 95-day circumnavigation of the globe leaving in January. Her clientele varied from millionaires on the long cruises to immigrants from Scandinavia, to Swedes travelling transatlantic to connect with one of her Caribbean cruises, to Nobel Prize-winners on their way to Stockholm.

When war broke out in the autumn of 1939, the *Kungsholm* was kept on the western side of the Atlantic for safety. She was sent on continuous West Indies cruises and, despite the harsh times, maintained her popularity with the American travelling public. However, this phase ended on December 13 1941, when she was officially seized by the United States government at her New York pier. She was the last foreign-flag liner operating commercially from the port and her requisition signalled the end of peace-time liner service for nearly four years. Several weeks later, on January 2, she was sold in New York by the representatives of the Swedish American Line to the American War Shipping Administration. The Stars and Stripes were hoisted and she was renamed USS *John Ericsson*, in tribute to the famed Swedish inventor-engineer who designed the USS *Monitor* of American Civil War fame. As a troop ship, she was listed with a capacity of 5,461 and sailed under the operational management of the United States Lines.

On her first trooping voyage, the *Ericsson* left New York in January 1942, passed through the Panama Canal and sailed to Melbourne and Noumea in the South Pacific. Next, after returning to Los Angeles and San Francisco for dry-docking, she travelled to Wellington, New Zealand, and then back to New York via Panama. There followed three return trips to Casablanca with invasion forces and then a long-haul run to Oran (North Africa), England, Freetown (West Africa), and Cape Town. On that transatlantic return, she was detoured to St John's, Newfoundland to receive troops transferred from the *Strathnaver*, a former P & O liner. During all of 1944 and 1945, and most of 1946, she worked on the North Atlantic, sailing either from New York or Boston to Southampton, Liverpool, Glasgow, Cherbourg, Le Havre, Marseilles, and, after the surrender, to Bremerhaven. An additional task came in 1946 when she was outfitted as a 'war bride' ship with special provisions for 279 mothers and 177 infants.

With her military work almost complete, misfortune struck in March 1947, while she was lying at her New York pier off West 50th Street. Fire started and spread quickly, resulting in considerable damage. Fortunately, however, there was no threat of capsizing as was the case with the *Normandie* five years before. Then, in a most surprising move and despite the damages, she was resold to her original owners, the Swedish American Line. However, the Brostrom family, owners of the line, had no intention of restoring her as the *Kungsholm*. Instead, in December, she sailed for Genoa and thorough reconditioning for the newly formed Home Lines, a company in which the Brostrom family had considerable interest. The new firm was an answer to the almost desperate post-war need for services for immigrants and displaced persons. Following some alterations, the ship was renamed *Italia* and entered the South American trade from Italian ports on July 27 1948. A year or so later, due to currency problems in Latin America, she was returned to the North Atlantic, sailing between Genoa and New York. Still later, in 1952, she was transferred to the Hamburg–Channel ports–Halifax–New York service and a final change in 1959 took her from north European ports to Quebec City and Montreal. Her lifeline at this time seems to have been basically low-fare tourists and immigrants on the westward sailings. The berthing plan was arranged for 213 in First Class and 1,106 in Tourist. She sailed under the Panamanian flag, mostly with Italian and German personnel.

The *Italia* was withdrawn in the autumn of 1960 and despatched to Genoa for a major facelift. A vast lido deck with two pools was built in the stern. Her cabins were improved and the public areas upgraded. Thereafter, the capacity was limited to 680, all First Class. In December of that year, she opened a new Home Lines' service, on weekly seven-day cruises between New York and Nassau, departing each Saturday, with a minimum fare of $170. It was an instant success and in less than five years the same service sustained the 39,000-ton, 1,200-passenger *Oceanic*. The *Italia* became extremely well known at this time and can be considered as one of the forerunners of the concept of year-round cruising, particularly for established Atlantic firms like the Home Lines. She was replaced in the spring of 1964 by the larger *Homeric* and then a year later by the brand new *Oceanic*.

After a brief turn in dry dock, the *Italia* was sold for £446,000 to Freeport Bahama Enterprise Limited, a newly created business group. Her purpose was that of a floating hotel in Freeport, Grand Bahama, a location then very much in the throes of rapid expansion for tourism. She was rechristened *Imperial Bahama Hotel* and listed as having accommodation for 1,400 guests (passengers).

This scheme flopped within a year, despite the $1,000,000 spent on improvements to the ship. The operation was clouded in scandals, high-lighted by one charging embezzlement on the part of the management. The Bahamian government was quick to intercede and as a result the ship was put on the auction block to recover debts. The highest bidder offered £265,000 and was immediately accepted. An ocean-going tug assisted and, on September 8 1965, she arrived with the liner in tow in Bilbao, Spain. Within months, the old *Kungsholm* was scrapped.

Gross tonnage: 20,223
Length overall: 609 feet
Width: 78 feet
Draft: 29 feet
Machinery: Burmeister & Wain Diesels geared to twin screw
Speed: 17 knots
Capacity: 115 First, 490 Second, 970 Third
Built: Blohm & Voss Shipbuilders A/G, Hamburg, Germany, 1928
Demise: Scrapped in Bilbao, Spain, 1965

Above *The* Kungsholm *under her Swedish American colours. After 1932 she was painted with a white hull* (Courtesy of Roger Scazzafava).

Below *Renamed* John Ericsson, *she served as a US troop ship in the Second World War.*

"JOHN ERICSSON"

Above *Sold to Home Lines after the war she was renamed* Italia. *This photo shows her at Kingston, in the 1950s.*
Below and right *A black band on the top of her stacks was added in her last years as a Home liner.*

Fifty Famous Liners

Bremen

In 1920, the Germans were just about stripped of all passenger ships, including the spectacular Hamburg America Line trio of giants (*Imperator, Vaterland,* and *Bismarck*) and all but one practically unuseable four-stacker from the North German Lloyd fleet. At the end of World War 1, the Allied Reparations Commission decided to allow the 32,000-ton *Columbus*, which was idle and untouched at Danzig, to be completed for her original North German Lloyd owners. (Her earlier sister ship, the intended *Columbus*, was given over to the White Star Line to become their *Homeric*.) This second *Columbus*, although laid down as the *Hindenburg* in 1914, and despite the apparent need for German passenger traffic wanting to travel in a national ship, was delayed in its final construction by labour and material shortages and other problems, until April 1924. The Germans were slowly reopening their North-Atlantic passenger operations. The Lloyd's chief rival, the Hamburg America Line, decided in view of the new American immigration quotas that they would rebuild only with medium-sized passenger ships of the 21,000-ton *Albert Ballin* type.

North German Lloyd were pleased with the operating results of the *Columbus* and were encouraged enough to consider two further 35,000-ton, 775-foot liners for a weekly service using three ships similar to the Cunard and White Star Lines. These British firms were of course in the dominant position during the 1920s, particularly with the blazing glory of the *Mauretania*, the fastest passenger liner afloat since 1907. The Germans were envious,

just as they had been when they attempted to gain world prestige in 1913–14 with the first of Ballin's Hamburg America superships. Somewhere, shortly after 1927, the concept of those two additional 35,000-tonners changed, even after the keel had been laid, to 50,000-ton speed queens that would successfully challenge both the *Mauretania* herself and Britain's supreme transatlantic role.

The finest German designers and engineers competed for the honour of designing these new floating symbols of their nation. The hulls came off the drawing-boards as long and sleek, and with rounded stems that supposedly added speed. However, most novel of all was the introduction of the bulbous bow, a rounded underwater stem which greatly reduced drag at sea and which had the effect of keeping the bow section from plunging too deeply at sea and also of keeping the four propellers under water in rough weather. The overall exterior design called for long, slender hulls, topped by an orderly and well-arranged superstructure with twin pear-shaped mustard-coloured funnels (the *Europa*'s were oval-shaped) that were exceptionally squat in height. Two towering masts balanced the general silhouette.

As the designers and shipbuilding crews worked, the publicists in conjunction with fiercely determined government ministers, who were financing the project to a great extent, produced a master plan: the two liners would cross to New York on their voyages together as they took the record from Britain's *Mauretania*. The impression on the world,

symbolic both of German recovery and technological ability, would be startling, it was estimated.

The *Europa* was launched first, on August 15 1928, at the Blohm & Voss yards of Hamburg, in the presence of President Hindenburg. The *Bremen* followed a day later, at the Weser Shipyards in Bremen. All seemed to be following the master plan. Then, on March 26, in the following spring, the *Europa* was swept by fire at the shipyards. She would be delayed by at least a year. Consequently, as *Bremen* progressed on schedule, the fate of the two ships altered somewhat. She left Bremerhaven on July 16 1929, on a triumphant crossing to New York, immediately capturing the Atlantic Blue Riband, with a run from Cherbourg to the Ambrose Light, at an average 27.83 knots (against the *Mauretania*'s 26.6, dating from September 1909). The *Bremen*'s passage represented 4 days, 17 hours, and 42 minutes. The veteran *Mauretania* tried once more, registering an incredible 27.2 knots against her 22 years of age, but in the end could not really succeed and instead sent warmest congratulations to her Germanic successor. Berlin was rightly proud of its accomplishment.

The *Bremen* made headline news around the world and was thereafter firmly secured as the better known and more popular of the sisters. Although the *Europa* captured the Blue Riband herself in March 1930, the title eventually went back to the *Bremen* before passing to the Italian, *Rex*, in the summer of 1933.

The North German Lloyd publicists worked a most interesting campaign to keep these German greyhounds in the news. Just after their completion, a Lufthansa seaplane was placed in a revolving catapult that rested between the twin stacks. Approximately 40 hours before reaching either shore, the plane was loaded with mail and despatched ahead, creating something of a sea-air mail service. Although the concept certainly attracted considerable press attention, in fact it was a costly, awkward procedure. As one example, the plane had to be lifted by a large, heavy-duty floating crane back to its catapult at both Bremerhaven and New York. The operation was discontinued by 1935. In another case, the publicists achieved the best possible response to a rather bothersome situation. Upon their completion, the *Bremen* and *Europa* were unable to dock at any of the passenger-ship piers along Manhattan's west shore. Although new facilities were under construction, they were temporarily forced to use the Brooklyn Army Terminal, which is about five miles south of the New York City area and quite near to the Lower Bay and opening to the Atlantic itself. For passengers unhappy with the extra taxi ride to that distant pier, the Lloyd responded with, 'You are that much closer to Europe when you sail on the *Bremen* or *Europa*!'

Both of the sisters were more popular with German passengers than with any others including Americans. When brand new, they suffered from anti-German feelings, a result of World War 1. Later, in the 1930s, as the Nazi machine grew, they again lost potential clientele. However, as official 'ships of state', just as the *Rex* was to Italy or the *Normandie* to France, their creation was not based upon even the wildest dreams of profitability but on the concept of grandiose ornaments of national pride and ability.

The *Bremen* undertook several winter cruises around the world during her decade of commercial service. They took her to such places as Rio, the Suez Canal, Bombay, the East Indies, California, and Hawaii. She also gained the honour of being the largest liner to transit both the Panama and Suez Canals, a title snatched from the *Empress of Britain* and left unchallenged until record passages by the *Queen Elizabeth 2*, in the early 1970s.

The *Bremen* was at her New York pier on August 28 1939. Her captain and crew were anxious to return to Germany before war was declared. The United States coastguard decided to detain the ship a further two days, supposedly checking for munitions going aboard. With final clearance and authorities unable to press for further delay, the liner was allowed to sail, without passengers, for her homeland. Her orders were for strictest caution. At sea, she was 'blacked out' at night and had been repainted in grey for camouflage during daylight. She sailed to Murmansk, where she arrived on September 6, on a far more northern course than she would have normally taken. As war began, she remained in hiding, seeking refuge in fogbanks and clinging closely to the Norwegian coastline. At one point, she even hoisted the Soviet colours as a precaution. She managed to survive and on December 13 reached Bremerhaven.

Alongside her sister, she was painted in one of those extraordinary 'dazzle' effects, presumably for use at sea. Information leaked that the pair were being outfitted to carry military personnel for the invasion of the north-east coast of Britain, as part of Hitler's Operation Sea Lion. It was estimated that the *Bremen* and *Europa* could transport thousands of invasion troops from a base in Norway. Huge off-loading doors were cut into the sides of each liner and materials for the handling of 10–15,000 soldiers per trip went aboard. The *Bremen* was sent to Hamburg to complete her military refit. Then, quite suddenly, the work stopped and she was returned to Bremer-haven and used as an accommodation ship. She was never to sail again.

On a quiet Sunday afternoon, March 16 1941, an unhappy cabin boy started a fire in a storeroom. The *Bremen* was practically unguarded and fire-fighting crews were totally unprepared. She burned thoroughly and later listed heavily against her pier.

With the more urgent efforts of the Nazi Movement, the *Bremen* was considered beyond repair. Scrappers went aboard and some of her salvaged steel was sent off to munitions factories. At the end of the war her last remains were taken to the lower part of the River Weser and destroyed with explosives. With the *Europa* seized by the American liberation forces, Germany had once again lost its greatest liners.

Gross tonnage: 51,656 (1929), 51,731 (1937)
Length overall: 938 feet
Width: 102 feet
Draft: 34 feet
Machinery: Steam turbines geared to quadruple screw
Speed: 27 knots
Capacity: 800 First, 500 Second, 300 Tourist, 600 Third
Built: A G Weser Shipbuilders, Bremen, Germany, 1929
Demise: Destroyed by fire on March 16 1941; later scrapped

Right *The hot July day on which the* Bremen *first docked at her pier in Brooklyn.*
Below *The new speed queen had a strikingly fresh silhouette.*

Fifty Famous Liners

Bremen

Above *Note the aeroplane on its catapult between the* Bremen's *twin stacks. See how the black soot is coming from the ship's forward funnel.*

Below *With her stacks raised substantially, she still looked magnificent. Here she is docking in Cherbourg in 1934.*

Asama Maru

At the time of their construction in 1928, the sister ships *Asama Maru* and *Tatsuta Maru* of Nippon Yusen Kaisha—the NYK Line—were the largest Japanese liners ever built. Furthermore, they were the first big motor ships built for that country. As a team, they signified advances on the transpacific run in the form of accelerated service, greater luxury, and stiffer competition to the American-flag and Canadian Pacific fleets, which had long dominated that service.

The *Asama Maru* was the slightly more interesting sister. She was launched at the Mitsubishi Shipbuilding Yard in Nagasaki on October 30 1928 and left Yokohama on her maiden voyage to San Francisco on the following October 10. The *Tatsuta Maru* joined in April 1930. Their popularity developed quickly, particularly among Japanese passengers.

They were a fitting pair as Japan's newest and largest liners. For expert navigation, there was a radio direction finder, a gyro compass and two motorised lifeboats fitted with radio and searchlights. In addition, there were 20 other boats which could more than adequately handle the entire passenger and crew complements. There was space for 7,000 tons of cargo plus 300 tons listed as 'express cargo' and a further 300 in refrigerated compartments.

The passenger accommodation was divided into 239 First, 96 Second, and 504 Third Class. The First-Class section included a boat deck aft verandah, with walls done in imitation stone and with chairs, tables and settees that gave an overall Spanish patio effect. Adjoining was the Japanese room, done in tokonoma and with thick tatami floor covering. It was an exact replica of the interior of a Japanese house. Japanese foods—such as sukiyaki—were served here to further the authentic amosphere. The main stairwell encircled a complete working fountain. Other public rooms included: the library and writing room, done in period English style; the main lounge in Georgian style, complete with glass-domed ceiling; the smoking room and bar in Tudor style, with a beamed ceiling and a deep fireplace; and the main dining saloon, done in mahogany with black marble columns. The Pompeian indoor swimming pool had its own domed ceiling and adjoined a complete gymnasium. The dining rooms for all classes were serviced by electrically equipped kitchens.

The *Asama Maru* had the fine profile of the contemporary motorliner: rather long and slender with evenly spaced, almost squat-like funnels. At first, her stacks were painted entirely in black but were later given the twin-red and triple-white bands of the NYK Line.

Apart from the *Asama Maru* and her sister, the *Tatsuta Maru*, there was a third, distinct unit, the 17,400-ton *Chichibu Maru*. In addition to Japanese immigrants seeking passage to the United States, the First-Class sections were often filled by businessmen, members of the diplomatic corps, traders, missionaries, and ordinary Orient-bound tourists. The service prospered.

However, in 1937, misfortune struck the *Asama Maru*. On September 2 she was docked at the Taikoo Shipyards in Hong Kong when a serious hurricane warning was received. She was moved, with the

intent of better protection, to an alcove in Saiwan Bay. The hurricane was harsher than anticipated. Fierce wind forces snapped the liner's anchor chains and tossed her ashore, resulting in a list in a rather deserted area of the harbour. The prospect of refloating seemed most difficult. The Nippon Salvage Company was contracted and sent work boats and crews from Japan. The initial theory that high tide would float the ship's hull sufficiently to free her proved incorrect. The task was far more complicated. The 16,900-ton liner had to be made lighter. Consequently, barges were moored alongside and 3,500 tons of material were slowly removed. This included two of the four main engines. She was freed finally in March 1938, six months later. Repairs were made in Japan and included the reinsertion of the items removed in Hong Kong. She was back in service, leaving Yokohama on September 15.

The NYK liners remained in commercial service through 1940, well beyond most of their European counterparts on the transatlantic run. In 1941, the Asama Maru was converted to a transport, sailing for the Japanese Navy. Little is known about her movements but it can be safely said that they were confined to the western Pacific and, in all probability, limited to service between Japanese ports and mainland Asia. Her end came on November 1 1944 when she was torpedoed and sunk by the United States submarine *Atule*, in a position 100 miles south of Pratas Island in the China Sea. By the end of the war the Japanese were left with one passenger ship.

Gross tonnage: 16,975
Length overall: 583 feet
Width: 71 feet
Machinery: Sulzer diesels geared to quadruple screw
Speed: 21 knots
Capacity: 239 First, 96 Second, 504 Third
Built: Mitsubishi Shipbuilding Company, Nagasaki, Japan, 1929
Demise: Torpedoed and sunk in the China Sea, November 1 1944

The launching of the Asama Maru *on October 30 1928.*

Above left *The First-Class lounge brought a new standard of elegance to the Pacific.* **Above right** *The bedroom of a de luxe suite.* **Below** Asama Maru *arriving at Pier 36, San Francisco.*

Europa/Liberté

The *Europa*—with her near-sister *Bremen* (one of the slight differences was that the *Bremen* was two feet longer)—were scheduled to go into North Atlantic service together on April 1 1929. Their impact on the world was expected to be enormous, affecting luxury-liner design, machinery, and speed, and generally reflecting in a positive way Germany's post-World War 1 recovery. However, the *Europa* was destined for some misfortune. A major strike by workers at the Blohm & Voss Hamburg yards began on October 28 1928 and lasted until January 29. Although all of the specialist managers continued their tasks, the completion of the ship could no longer be assured for the North German Lloyd's intended date. Then, even greater problems arose.

Fire broke out on board the incomplete liner on March 25 and spread rapidly, especially destroying and buckling the upper-deck areas. Some 350 firemen using 65 hoses fought the blaze well into the next day but, as feared, the inevitable occurred: she sank at her berth. Initial inspections by her designers and the shipyard crews listed her as beyond repair and suitable only for salvage and then scrapping. However, further appraisals showed that she could be saved. Consequently, on April 10, she was raised and major repairs began. An additional ten months were required for completion.

The *Europa* finally left Bremerhaven on March 19 1930 on her maiden crossing to New York. Despite her initial difficulties, she proved to be a tribute to her makers by capturing the Blue Riband from the *Bremen* with a recorded 27.91 knots between Cherbourg and Ambrose. Ultimately, the latter ship recaptured the Riband in June 1933, after modifications to her machinery, with an average of 28.51 knots.

The record standing of these German liners remained supreme until the Italian *Rex* snatched the Blue Riband in August 1933. Later, in 1935, France's *Normandie* appeared as not only faster but bigger and more luxurious, and finally the *Queen Mary* firmly brought the speed honours back to Britain. The North German Lloyd, prodded by the Berlin government, was anxious to reinstate its position of supremacy on the Atlantic. Thought was given to re-engining the *Bremen* and the *Europa* in order to produce speeds that would outstep both the *Normandie* and the *Queen Mary*. Another scheme was to build two larger superliners, again with amazingly high speed capabilities. However, in the end, nothing went beyond the drawing board stages.

On June 29 1937, in the North Sea, the *Europa* rescued three crewmen from the sinking German tanker *Olifer*. Ten others were lost in the tragedy.

On a westbound crossing, in late August 1939, the *Europa* was about to head into the Atlantic when she was ordered to return to her home port. Blacked out and with radio silence, she reversed course and, amidst great anxiety, off-loaded her passengers back onto the dockside in Bremerhaven. A few days later war began. She was repainted grey and used as a permanently stationed accommodation centre for navy crews. During 1940, she sailed to Hamburg—just as the *Bremen* had done—and was to be converted for use in the intended sea invasion of Britain. Within a short time, the concept was abandoned and the former liner returned to Bremerhaven. She was nearby when, in March 1941, her former running-mate was destroyed by fire, but remained unharmed. She moved to the position of largest German passenger ship. In 1942, a rumour had her scheduled for massive conversion to an aircraft-carrier, in a process used by the Italians and Japanese on some of their passenger ships.

The *Europa* was a neglected, rusting sight when the American forces reached Bremerhaven in May 1945. Somehow, she managed to remain afloat throughout the later war years and despite orders from the retreating Nazi high command to sink her at the pier. Internally, there were signs of some troop provision but for voyages she never made. She was put under the United States flag and designated AP-177, USS *Europa*.

She was given some temporary repairs (and later dry-docked in New York harbour) before beginning American troop service in September. Her capacity was listed at 4,300 with 900 crew. However, she was plagued by small fires caused, it was determined, by the removal of her original high-quality fittings and their replacement with inferior items by the Germans in order to compensate for material shortages as their war effort began to regress.

Furthermore, some serious hull cracks were uncovered, which worried authorities concerned with safety. The *Europa*'s spell of service as a US troop ship was short-lived. In early 1946, she was handed over to the Reparations Commission.

The French had the strongest need for a large passenger liner, having lost the *Normandie* in 1942. They were anxious to re-establish something of their luxurious pre-war passenger service and, it was thought, with proper modifications the *Europa* could be made to appear French. Consequently, she crossed to Le Havre and had her funnels repainted in French Line red and black. At first, the name *Lorraine* was intended but in the final decision *Liberté* seemed more apt.

Then more misfortune struck, on December 8 1946, as the *Liberté* was pulled from her moorings, slammed into the wreck of the liner *Paris* (sunk in 1939 and not yet salvaged due to the war), and settled in Le Havre harbour. She had a large gash in her hull but fortunately remained in an upright position. The refit ceased as salvage took priority.

She was refloated by the spring, on April 15, and towed to the Chantiers de l'Atlantique Shipyard in St Nazaire, the birthplace of so many great French liners. Her $19,000,000 restoration programme finally began. There were more tense moments, in October 1949, when a fire damaged some of the fresh passenger interiors and caused further delay.

The *Liberté* arrived in New York on August 17 1950, as the 'new' flagship of French Line (the 'Transat', to the French themselves—an abbreviation of the firm's full title, Compagnie Générale Transatlantique). She was paired with the famous *Ile de France*, and later with the smaller *Flandre*, a 20,000-ton ship completed in 1952. The larger ship's tonnage had increased from her German days, from 49,746 to 51,839, and for some time she was listed as the world's fourth largest liner after the *Queen Elizabeth*, the *Queen Mary*, and the *United States*. After 1954, when her original stacks were fitted with dome tops, she could boast two of the mightiest funnels afloat.

The 66,000-ton *France* was ordered in 1956, with delivery estimated for late 1961, and was intended to replace both the *Liberté* and the *Ile de France*. Just as the transatlantic liner trade began to decline in its battle with aircraft travel in 1958, the *Ile* was retired. Three years later, in November 1961, the *Liberté* left New York in a gala farewell departure. Briefly, in Le Havre, she was berthed close to her successor, then nearing completion.

At first, there were rumours that she would become a floating hotel for the 1962 World's Fair in Seattle. Two liners, the former British *Dominion Monarch* and the Mexican *Acapulco*, were later used for this purpose since, in the end, French Line was fearful of some 'undignified' end for its former flagship. It recalled what had happened to the *Ile de France* at the hands of Hollywood film-makers in 1959. The *Liberté* was sold to the India Shipping and Trading Company of Vaduz, Leichtenstein, an intermediary firm, with the clear stipulation that French Line should have control over her final days. She was resold, according to plan, to ship-breakers in La Spezia, Italy, and arrived there on January 30 1962. By June she was gone forever.

Gross tonnage: 49,746 (1930), 51,839 (1950)
Length overall: 936 feet
Width: 102 feet
Draft: 34 feet
Machinery: Steam turbines geared to quadruple screw
Speed: 27 knots
Capacity: 687 First, 524 Second, 306 Tourist, 507 Third (1930); 569 First, 562 Cabin, 382 Tourist (1950)
Built: Blohm & Voss Shipbuilders A/G, Hamburg, Germany, 1930
Demise: Scrapped in La Spezia, Italy, 1962

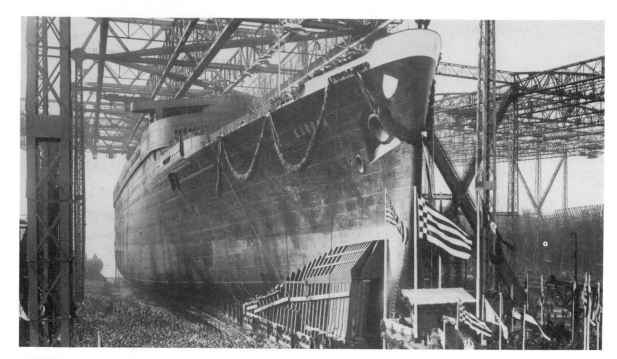

Above left *Even at her launching the* Europa *projected a feeling of greatness and excitement.*

Left *The new twin flyers together in Bremerhaven.*

Above *The* Europa *digs her nose into heavy Atlantic seas.*

Right *Seized intact, the* Europa *was pressed into troop ship service, becoming the USS* Europa.

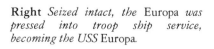

Above *Sunk in Le Havre while the French were rebuilding her. She was a sorry sight! Note French Line stack markings.*

Below *Once again the last word—now renamed the* Liberté—*she lies between the new* United States, *the* Georgic *(partly hidden), the* Queen Mary, *and the* Media.

Empress of Britain

The Canadian Pacific Company had the reputation of 'spanning the world'—transatlantic from Britain to eastern Canada, by rail across the continent, and then transpacific from Vancouver to the Orient. The entire operation was most successful and convenient. A good-sized fleet of large and often fast passenger ships created the marine division which was headed by the famed *Empress* liners. In the mid-1920s, plans were drawn for new flagships for both the Atlantic and Pacific services that were both larger and faster than any previously seen. The transpacific queen was launched as *Empress of Japan* in December 1929. She was 26,000 tons and, within a year of completion, made the fastest run ever between Vancouver and Yokohama. Her success was assured until the outbreak of World War 2.

The second ship was designed for the more prestigious transatlantic trade and was therefore larger and faster still, in keeping with the standards already established by the superliners servicing the New York trade. However, this ship had a further, quite novel purpose: she was intended to lure American and Canadian passengers from the west and mid-west to sail in her via Quebec City rather than through the more customary port of New York. Therefore, her design and decoration were specifically intended to make her something of a serious contender to the Manhattan-based liners. She was quite appropriately christened *Empress of Britain*, on June 11 1930, by the then very popular Prince of Wales (later the Duke of Windsor). For the first time the launch proceedings were broadcast throughout the British Empire.

Built by the well-established John Brown yards of Clydebank, Scotland, she was Britain's biggest liner since the 45,600-ton *Aquitania*, completed in 1914. Her hull was strengthened for ice in view of her more northern voyages to the St Lawrence region. She had five cargo holds—the first three for general cargo, the fourth for insulated goods, and the fifth for passenger baggage. Her designer opted for mammoth, almost overpowering funnels, which at first opposed Canadian Pacific's desire for more normal-sized stacks. In the end, the designer got his way. Together with the smart, sleek hull and super-structure, the three giant funnels added greatly to the overall illusion of grandeur. In daylight, her appearance was most handsome—certainly she was one of the grandest liners of the 1930s period. At night, with the three stacks floodlit, her appearance was even more dramatic.

Her interiors were noteworthy and represented a mixture of styles. The Mayfair Lounge was traditional, in contrast with the modern decor of the Cathay Lounge, for example. The Salle Jacques Cartier was quickly established as one of the finest restaurants afloat, while the Empress Ballroom and The Mall were equally well-known shipboard rooms. There was a large indoor swimming pool and a popular squash court located on the highest deck.

The *Empress of Britain* left Southampton on her maiden voyage to Quebec City on May 27 1931. She was certainly unlike any previous passenger liner on the Canadian trade and therefore attracted considerable attention. She was, without question, the fastest. Her best run came in August 1934, between Father Point and Cherbourg, with a record

of 4 days, 6 hours, and 58 minutes, averaging 25.08 knots. However, she was never a serious challenger to the Blue Riband liners of the day.

The *Empress* was built with the intention of sailing on the Atlantic between May and November, with the remaining time spent on an annual four-month around-the-world cruise. Each January, she would sail from New York, with her outer propellers removed to save fuel and drag, for the Mediterranean, pass through the Suez Canal, then on to India and the Dutch East Indies, to Hong Kong, China and Japan, then across to the Hawaiian islands, California, and transit the Panama Canal before returning. Her capacity for these cruises, which were bywords in travel for that time, was reduced from 1,195 to approximately 700. Considering her 42,000 tons, this rendered an unparalleled amount of space per passenger. Average fares for these trips began at $2,000.

However, while the *Empress of Britain* brought attention and honours to the Canadian Pacific fleet, she did not have winning results financially. On the North Atlantic, she was unable to attract enough passengers from the west. The general sea-going public preferred the established route of sailing from New York. Then, sadly, her operations were further complicated by the lack of an adequate running-mate that could assist in providing something of a weekly service in both directions. Her great speed and size placed her in a position well above all the other Canadian Pacific liners. On the world-cruise circuit, she was equally unprofitable. These voyages, sailing in the peak years of the Depression, were often listed in the red. The glorious *Empress* was one of the least profit-making liners of her day. In July 1935, when a rumour persisted that Canadian Pacific was planning to build a sister ship, the owners could only cite, in response, the economic infeasibility of such a project. (Even after the war, when Canada offered to build a similar-sized replacement as a gift to Canadian Pacific for its outstanding war-time services, the opportunity was graciously declined.)

The *Empress* and the 5,100-ton British freighter, *Kafiristan*, collided in fog, in the Atlantic, on June 16 1935. The smaller vessel was seriously damaged and caught fire while the liner suffered only minor injury to her starboard bow. After a lengthy inquiry in London, it was determined that the larger ship was 75 per cent to blame.

Their Majesties King George VI and Queen Elizabeth (later Her Majesty Queen Elizabeth, the Queen Mother) travelled home in the *Empress of Britain* from their successful tour of North America in June 1939. The royal couple had sailed outward one month before in the *Empress of Australia.*

The *Empress of Britain* left Southampton on September 2 1939, the day after the Nazi invasion of Poland, with far more than her normal load of passengers. Evacuees and desperate tourists without actual cabin accommodation were given cots in the public rooms and in a special arrangement in the squash court. At Quebec City, she was temporarily laid up pending further decisions by the British government. In November, she was officially requisitioned for transport work and was repainted in grey. She docked in Clydebank, in December, to be fully outfitted as a troop ship, and then quickly afterwards made two further Canadian sailings, bringing some of the first servicemen from that country for the war effort. In March 1940 she was ordered to New Zealand. Briefly, she sailed in convoy with the *Queen Mary*, the *Aquitania*, and others equally far removed from their intended peace-time trades. Her spell in the southern climates was quite short, however.

The *Empress* was returning home to England, via Cape Town and Freetown, on October 26, when she was attacked and set afire by Nazi aircraft bombers when only 70 miles north-west of Ireland. One of the bombs made a direct hit on the site of the Mayfair Lounge. All but 49 of her more than 600 passengers and crew were saved. The blistered and burnt hulk was put under tow by the Polish destroyer *Burza*. Two days later, on the 28th, the enemy submarine *U-32* sighted the former liner and fired two torpedoes. The *Empress* quickly sank. In the final accounting, she became the largest Allied merchant ship to be lost in World War 2.

Gross tonnage: 42,348
Length overall: 758 feet
Width: 97 feet
Machinery: Steam turbines geared to quadruple screw
Speed: 24 knots
Capacity: 465 First, 260 Tourist, 470 Third
Built: John Brown & Company Limited, Clydebank, Scotland, 1931
Demise: Torpedoed and sunk off Ireland, October 28 1940

Right *Launching in Clydebank on June 11 1930.*

Below *Crowds watch the giant new Empress depart for her sea-trials on April 4 1931.*

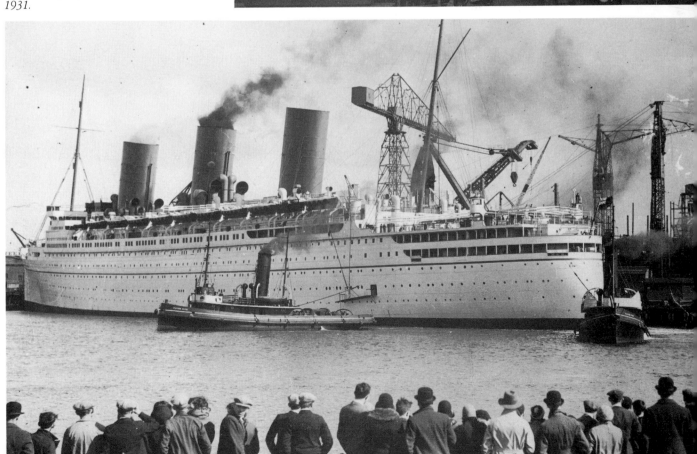

Left *In Southampton: the* Empress of Britain, *the* Olympic, *and the* Berengaria.

Right *The* Empress *entering King George V Graving Dock in Southampton November 17 1937. White Star's* Laurentic *is laid up to the left.*

Left *The modern Cathay Room was one of the most interesting rooms afloat.*

Fifty Famous Liners

Empress of Britain

Monarch of Bermuda

Many passenger ships have endured extremely varied lives in regard to the services they provide, the owners they serve and the modifications which they undergo. One such ship was the British liner *Monarch of Bermuda*. She has left behind an unusually diverse history made up of four different phases of life: Bermuda cruise ship, war-time transport, Australian immigrant ship, and trans-atlantic passenger liner.

The *Monarch* was under construction in 1931 for the Furness Bermuda Line at the Vickers-Armstrongs' yard of Newcastle, England. She was designed as the new, large consort to the highly popular *Bermuda*, a ship completed in 1927 and one which saw the New York–Bermuda cruise trade become a year-round, highly successful one. The new ship was to have been called *Mid-Ocean* but, suddenly, there was a change of plan. The *Bermuda* was burnt out at her Hamilton pier in June 1931 and then again at a Belfast repair yard. The Furness Company was forced to rely on chartered ships, at least temporarily, such as Cunard's *Franconia*, Holland-America's *Veendam*, and the *Duchess of Bedford* of Canadian Pacific. The new liner, still being built in Newcastle, now became a much-needed replacement. The Furness image needed boosting and the more glamorous name, *Monarch of Bermuda*, was selected.

The new liner was an immediate success, following her maiden voyage in December 1931, which led to the decision to build a sister, the *Queen of Bermuda* of 1933.

The accommodation on board the *Monarch* (and also the *Queen of Bermuda*) was of a particularly notable standard for the period. Every passenger cabin was fitted with a private toilet and bath or shower and the entire ship was of a 'First Class only' specification. However, it should be noted that the *Monarch*'s capacity of 831 was planned so as to allow the addition of a Second Class of 31 passengers if desired. As a team, the two liners were known as the 'millionaires' ships', due to their high quality facilities, and were capable of carrying 4,500 passengers to and from Bermuda every three weeks.

The *Monarch* had a pleasing appearance with three evenly slanted funnels, the third of which was a 'dummy'. She was fitted with turbo-electric machinery, which was an unusual system but a type that was eventually selected by the French for the *Normandie* in 1935. Turbo-electricity had two substantial benefits for the Furness sisters: greater service speed (19½ knots) and easier manoeuvrability. Another unique aspect of the design was that the size of the 22,500-ton hulls were greatly minimised in regard to length and draught. As a result, the ratio of beams to the length was slightly more than seven to one.

The *Monarch of Bermuda* attracted considerable attention in September 1934 as one of the chief rescue ships when the American liner *Morro Castle* burned off the New Jersey coast.

In November 1939, she was requisitioned for war service and returned to Britain for outfitting as a transport. Her appearance was changed to drab grey. Her records indicate but one of those 'near escapes' during war-time. While on a voyage from Norway, with over 2,000 troops on board, she became the

target for enemy aircraft. Utilising her top speed, she was able to seek safety in a dense fog bank before the actual attack began. Subsequently, the *Monarch* transported military, naval, and RAF contingents to the Near East and proved very valuable during the African and Italian invasion campaigns. Fortunately, she emerged from the war with relatively minor battle scars.

On March 24 1947 tragedy struck. While in Newcastle, undergoing her post-war refit for return to the Bermuda trade, she was swept by fire. The damage was extensive and her owners abandoned interest. The crippled hulk was towed to the Firth of Forth and laid up. The scrapyard seemed her most obvious fate. Then, due to the Ministry of Transport's desperate need for passenger spaces, the British government arranged to buy the ship. She was again put under tow and brought to Southampton for thorough repairs and rebuilding at the Thornycroft Shipyard.

She was rechristened *New Australia* and emerged as a new ship. Her original three funnels were replaced by one conventional funnel, plus a special dipod mast from which smoke was also dispersed. The accommodation—although of a very austere nature—was more than doubled from the original design, resulting in 1,593 berths in a single class. Although owned by the government, she was managed by the passenger department of Shaw Savill Line. On August 15 1950, she took up her new life as an immigrant ship, departing from Southampton for Australia via Suez.

With the eventual decline of the Australian migrant trade by ship, the *New Australia* became superfluous and was sold off in January 1958 to the Greek Line (the Arcadia Steamship Corporation) which sent her to the Blohm & Voss Shipyard in Hamburg for a major refit prior to normal passenger service. Externally, her hull was repainted in white and a new bow fitted that increased the overall length from 579 to 590 feet. Her accommodation was re-arranged as 150 First Class and 1,150 Tourist Class.

Monarch of Bermuda *photographed at Newcastle-upon-Tyne, where she was built, ready to make her maiden voyage on the service between New York and Bermuda.*

Monarch of Bermuda

Officially renamed *Arkadia*, she entered service in May 1958 between Bremerhaven, Amsterdam, London, Le Havre, Cóbh, Quebec City, and Montreal. In addition, there were winter cruise sailings, first from New York and later from Boston to Bermuda, the Bahamas, and the Caribbean. This winter operation later transferred to Southampton for sailings to the Canaries, Portugal and West Africa.

Until 1966, the *Arkadia* was seemingly unaffected by the aircraft competition that invaded the North Atlantic. The trade to eastern Canada was by then quickly declining and more time was allocated to pleasure-cruising. In November of that year, she was laid up in the River Fal. Her owners had given thought to a major reconstruction for year-round cruises but then her age, coupled with the cost, killed the idea. She was offered for sale but again her age of

35 was probably the greatest disadvantage. She left the Fal in December for the scrappers in Valencia, Spain—it seemed the only alternative. Most ironically, her one-time sister, *Queen of Bermuda*, was finishing her career at the same time, at the hands of ship-breakers in Faslane, Scotland. The *Monarch of Bermuda* had had a long and varied life.

Gross tonnage: 22,424
Length overall: 579 feet
Width: 76 feet
Draft: 26 feet
Machinery: Steam turbo-electric geared to quadruple screw
Speed: 19.5 knots
Capacity: 831 First or 800 First and 31 Second
Built: Vickers-Armstrong Limited, Newcastle, England, 1931
Demise: Scrapped in Valencia, Spain, 1966-7

A fine stern view of the Monarch of Bermuda; *she was burned in drydock on March 24 1947 while being refitted for her postwar return to the New York-Bermuda luxury run.*

Fifty Famous Liners

Above *Wearing warpaint in September 1939, the* Monarch of Bermuda *sails from New York for more hostile waters than she was accustomed to.*
Below *The Greek Line's* Arkadia *belies her age with her modern-looking profile.*

Rex

The three major Italian transatlantic lines—Cosulich, Lloyd Sabaudo, and Navigazione Generale Italiana (NGI)—had made tremendous progress during the 1920s in producing an outstanding fleet of passenger ships, all flying the national colours. This was Italy's great thrust in the Atlantic passenger trade. Prior to World War 1, the country had vessels of limited size and was not comparable to the progress and development made by such countries as England, Germany, France and even Holland. Therefore, the new ships of the 1920s represented Italy's serious bid for its share of the North-Atlantic liner business. Sufficient numbers of immigrants guaranteed profits in the vast, inexpensive Third-Class accommodation, but the Italian companies still hoped to lure First and Second-Class travellers to the Mediterranean route as opposed to the more customary northern route. For promotional purposes, the most attractive elements were the favourable 'southern route' climate and liners that could match the likes of the *Bremen*, the *Ile de France*, and even the older, more established types like the *Majestic* and the *Berengaria*.

Navigazione Generale Italiana had commissioned the 32,000-ton sisters, *Roma* and *Augustus*, in 1926-7, which were by far the largest, fastest and most luxurious Italian passenger liners yet built. Their success on the run to New York prompted the company to think in terms of yet a bigger vessel. The Italian government, itself thinking of the positive national image created by an extravagant ocean liner, assured a generous construction loan as well as an operating subsidy, supposedly given to transport mail and rated according to the ship's speed. The company and the government agreed that this new liner must not only be exceptionally well decorated, a floating reflection of Italian style, art, and history, but capable of wresting the prized Blue Riband from either the British or the Germans.

The new flagship was ordered from the Ansaldo Shipyard in Genoa. Simultaneously, its crack Italian-flag transatlantic competitor, Lloyd Sabaudo, announced plans for a major liner of its own that would come from the Cantieri Riuniti dell'Adriatico yards of Trieste. However, there was no specific competition between the two—NGI's liner would be the larger at 51,000 tons and would have the more powerful machinery, while Lloyd Sabaudo's ship would be somewhat smaller, at 48,000 tons, and would not be designed with the Blue Riband in mind.

King Victor Emmanuel III and Queen Elena attended the naming ceremony and launch of the new Italian supership, on August 1 1931. It pleased the royal couple that the name *Rex* was selected and was, in fact, a deliberate effort on the part of Premier Benito Mussolini to win further support among Italy's royalist factions. The previous suggestion to name the ship *Guglielmo Marconi* was abandoned by the Premier himself. At the launching, officials spoke optimistically of winning the Blue Riband within a year or so. Construction, which had already been accelerated, sped forth with even greater urgency.

Mussolini kept a close eye on the Atlantic passenger lines and finally felt, with further inducement from the ever-growing worldwide Depression, that the three principal lines should be merged to eliminate competition, cut costs, and to better coordinate sailing schedules. Thus, in January 1932, the Italian Line—or more simply 'Italia'—became the successor to the Cosulich, Lloyd Sabuado, and NGI lines. Suddenly, the *Rex* and her larger counterpart being built for Lloyd Sabaudo were destined to sail under the same houseflag, as running-mates.

Premier Mussolini attended a gala luncheon and toured the completed *Rex* just hours before her maiden departure from Genoa, on September 27 1932. Dressed in flags, to the sounds of saluting horns and sirens, and with a full passenger list of international celebrities that included New York's Mayor, Jimmy Walker, the liner sailed for her intended record-breaking crossing. She called at Villefranche and then headed westward. Then, suddenly, while approaching Gibraltar, fate overtook her: serious engine problems all but crippled the brand new ship. The Italian Line reported, with great embarrassment, that repairs would be made within hours; it would be a minor delay. Closer inspection found the fault to be more serious, one that would require at least a three-day stopover at the British colony. Many of the First-Class passengers grew impatient and left the liner. Mayor Walker travelled to Cherbourg and took the *Europa* for home. The Italians were mortified.

The *Rex* eventually continued her crossing to New York, but not without further mechanical complications. In Manhattan, she was forced to cancel her eastbound maiden sailing, rely on power from a floating railroad tender, and await parts from subsequent inbound Italian liners. The Blue Riband had to wait.

The *Rex* finally captured her intended prize, from the *Bremen*, almost a year later, in August 1933. She crossed with a recorded 28.92 knots against the German liner's 28.51 knots. The passage between Gibraltar and the Ambrose Light was now reduced to 4 days, 13 hours, and 58 minutes and would hold until the *Normandie*'s arrival in May 1935.

The *Rex* was acclaimed as a most beautiful ship and was particularly noted for her outdoor swimming pools and lido areas. Her owners worked diligently at stressing the benefits of the 'sunny southern route' to Europe. Multicoloured umbrellas were placed about the open decks, sand was scattered around the pool areas for a beach-like effect reminiscent of the French and Italian Rivieras, and most printed advertising concentrated on swim-suited passengers lolling about on vast sun-decks. The scheme had its appeal but did not succeed completely. The attempt to win over large portions of the Atlantic passenger trade from the northern-routed liners was not altogether successful. The *Rex* and her running-mates were left to rely more heavily on ethnic passengers, including westbound immigrants.

On one occasion, during a voyage to New York, the liner was tossed about in heavy seas for a full 12 hours, which left one crewman dead and many passengers injured. In March 1937, during high winds, she hit Manhattan's Pier 88 while undocking.

After September 1939, the *Rex* and her Italian fleet-mates were among the last foreign-flag ships to remain in transatlantic service, supposedly a symbol of Italy's continued neutrality. Service finally ended in the spring of 1940, just as the political situation was changing rapidly and the security of ships at sea could no longer be fully guaranteed. The *Rex* was laid up for safety in Bari, on the Adriatic coast. On August 15, following a change of plan, she was towed to Trieste. She never sailed again.

Various reports hinted that she was to be converted to an aircraft-carrier, similar to the plans for the *Roma* and *Augustus*, or to be used as a high-density transporter. Worst of all, the Nazi forces planned to use her as a blockade at the harbour entrance of Venice, sinking her deliberately so as to hinder the Allies. Nothing came to pass.

On September 8 1944, the anchored liner was sighted by RAF bombers and was hit with 123 rockets. She burst into flames over her entire length and, on the following day, rolled over and sank in the shallow waters of Capodistria, in the Gulf of Muggia, south of Trieste. At the end of the war, initial studies were made in the hope of salvaging the *Rex* but, in the same way that plans to refloat the *Normandie* in New York were thwarted by findings of damages beyond economic repair, the *Rex* was declared a total loss. Scrapping on the spot began in 1947, the final pieces being removed by June 1958. The Italians would never again build a faster passenger liner.

Gross tonnage: 51,062
Length overall: 879 feet
Width: 96 feet
Machinery: Steam turbines geared to quadruple screw
Speed: 28 knots
Capacity: 604 First, 378 Second, 410 Tourist, 866 Third
Built: Ansaldo Shipyards, Genoa, Italy, 1932
Demise: Burned and sunk during air attack near Trieste, Italy, September 8 1944; later scrapped on the spot 1947-58

Left *The towering bow and hull on the building ways in Genoa.*

Right *Crew members dangle in bo's'n chairs to keep the stacks all shining and fresh. This was hot work for the knees!*

Below *Berthed in New York in her maiden year.*

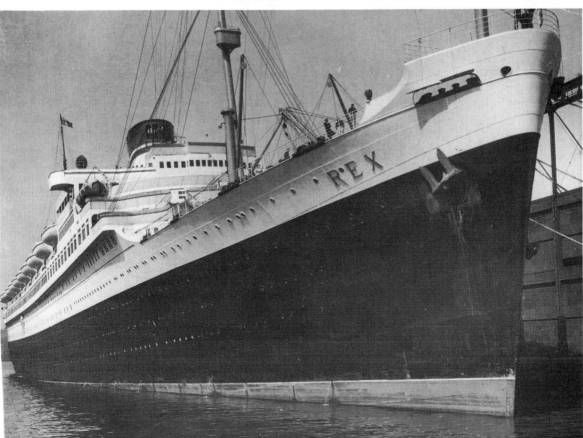

Above *On one of her final sailings from New York in the spring of 1940. The brand new* Queen Elizabeth, *painted in grey, rests at adjacent Pier 90.*

Left *A view of New York from the stern of the* Aquitania, *at the very beginning of war.*

Right *The great ship burning to death near Trieste, in September 1944.*

Rex

Conte di Savoia

When the Lloyd Sabaudo firmly decided to build a new passenger liner of major size and considerable decoration, they were not intent on achieving record-breaking speed. Quite simply, the distinctions of Italy's largest and fastest were left to the 51,000-ton *Rex*, being built for the rival Navigazione Generale Italiana. But the new Lloyd Sabaudo liner captured just as much interest and attention on the part of Premier Mussolini.

While the *Rex* was to be the record-breaker, this second ship was to be a blend of a modern profile and interiors of traditional stylings that would be a tour de force of Italian art and decoration. The immense Colonna Lounge was the classic example, done in marble with a great ceiling decorated in murals, high glass entrance doors, and tall figures on pedestals lining the port and starboard sides between the windows, facing onto the open deck and the sea beyond. Comparatively, it ranked as one of the great rooms aboard a luxury liner during the 1930s era and contrasted sharply with the more angular Art Deco effects of ships like the *Normandie*, the *Bremen*, and the *Queen Mary*.

The liner was christened *Conte di Savoia*, on October 28 1931, by the Princess of Piedmont. The name was selected, again by Mussolini, to honour and impress the ruling house of Savoy. The original choice was *Dux*, which was thought to be a suitable companion name to *Rex*, but this was changed to *Conte Azzuro* before the final selection was made. She was launched with a full weight of 18,730 tons and her owners noted that, while she was intended to sail to New York on the North Atlantic, she could be quite easily transferred to the South American service to Rio de Janeiro, Santos, Montevideo, and Buenos Aires.

Early in November 1932, she underwent her official trials and very pleasingly recorded a full 29.5 knots at one point. On the 30th, she left Genoa on her maiden run to New York. She was two months later than the *Rex*; nevertheless great attention was focused on her inaugural voyage. It seemed to pass quite well until, some 900 miles west of the American shore, an outlet valve below the waterline jammed and subsequently blew a worrisome hole in the side of the hull. In a matter of a few minutes seawater flooded the huge dynamo compartment. Reports were relayed to the bridge, and sensibly kept secret from her passengers, that the liner could sink in as little as five hours. Fortunately, the ship's engineers and crew were resourceful. One staff member—with near superhuman ability—succeeded in filling the open hole with cement. The *Conte di Savoia* was out of danger and, when the passengers were informed of the near tragedy, a handsome booty was passed to the heroic crewman.

Since both the *Rex* and the *Conte di Savoia* had difficult maiden voyages, suspicion was aroused as to whether their construction was too hurried as a result of pressures from the government and Mussolini himself, anxious to rival the other European maritime nations. In contrast with other great liners of the day, the Italian pair were completed in less than two years. In any event, the initial 'teething problems' were overcome and the two ships settled down to relatively trouble-free commercial careers.

While the *Rex* was larger and the proud holder of the Blue Riband, for publicity purposes the *Conte di Savoia* was known as the 'roll-less ship'. She was the first major liner and the very first of any type on the Atlantic to have the new gyro stabiliser system, a

balancing arrangement that pre-dates the fin stabiliser design which was perfected for passenger ships in the 1950s. Aboard the Italian liner, the gyro stabilisers were greatly publicised as being able to reduce the roll of the ship considerably and also restrict pitching. The concept was somewhat 'over sold' by the Italian Line, the newly created owner of the Lloyd Sabaudo fleet, in its press efforts during 1932–3. While the stabilisation system proved effective to some extent, it could not be used on any westbound crossings because prevailing winds could seriously jeopardise the ship's balance and therefore her safety. Passengers aboard the *Conte di Savoia* were sometimes surprised to find the ship tossing about just as any 'ordinary' Atlantic liner.

The *Conte di Savoia* continued her crossings to New York until the spring of 1940, along with the *Rex* and well beyond most other foreign passenger vessels. At the time of her last scheduled departure from the American port, the Italian Line director reported that 'both ships will resume sailings in September, when the war is over.' She was despatched to the Adriatic coast and laid up in Malamocco, near Venice. Just as with her larger running-mate, reports suggested that she might become an aircraft-carrier. She was used briefly as a transporter during 1943, but quickly returned to her safe anchorage at Malamocco. On September 11 of the same year she was sighted by Allied aircraft, attacked and set afire, and finally sank in shallow waters.

Her damaged hull was raised on October 16 1945 and, like all Italian liners sunk in home waters during the war, serious consideration was given to her resurrection. One design, considered the most likely, showed her rebuilt as an immigrant ship, with over 2,500 berths, all Third Class, few public rooms, and well over two dozen lifeboats. She was to be used on the Italy–South America route. The project hit snags: post-war material shortages, shortage of shipyard facilities, cost, and the caution required to tow her, in such an injured state, to a port for repairs. By 1950, the idea was abandoned and she was sold to local scrappers in Monfalcone.

Gross tonnage: 48,502
Length overall: 814 feet
Width: 96 feet
Machinery: Steam turbines geared to quadruple screw
Speed: 27 knots
Capacity: 500 First, 366 Second, 412 Tourist, 922 Third
Built: Cantieri Riuniti dell'Adriatico, Trieste, Italy, 1932
Demise: Sunk during air attack near Venice, September 11 1943; salvaged in 1945 and then scrapped by 1950

Oil is pumped aboard the Conte di Savoia *at Manhattan pier.*

Left *The* Conte di Savoia *off for Italy with a record passenger list—June 15 1933.*

Right *Sailing day—shortly after the start of Italy's war with Ethiopia—October 5 1935.*

Left *A photo of the great Italian liner taken in March 1939.*

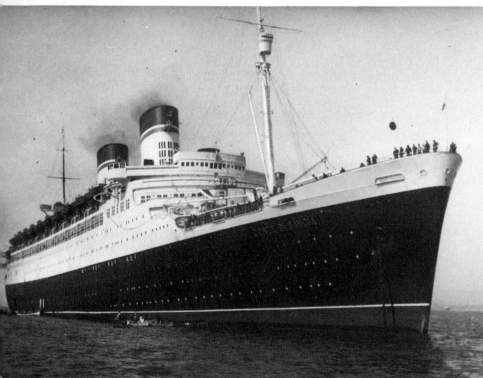

Conte di Savoia

Normandie

The *Normandie* was the ultimate ocean liner—definitely of the 1930s and possibly of the century. She was novel, innovative, glittering, and exceptionally advanced. She was the result of a continuing series of well-designed and highly decorated French Line passenger ships: the Louis XIV stylings of the *France* of 1912; the smartness of the *Paris* of 1921; the totally new styles of the *Ile de France* of 1926; and the modern profile of the *Champlain* of 1932. The *Normandie* took something from each of them and also from each of the other superships of the world. Her designers sought perfection and then went one step further, or so it would seem.

Her purpose was threefold: to be the world's largest liner (the first to exceed 1,000 feet in length and 60,000 tons), to be the fastest on the North Atlantic (although this was continuously denied by the French Line since the publicity damage would be shattering should she not, for some unexplained reason, manage to outpace the Italian *Rex* which then held the Blue Riband), and, thirdly, to be a dazzling floating centre of French art, decoration, and technology. The French government subsidised much of the $60 million construction, in itself by far the highest amount ever paid for a passenger liner,

and, in its foresight, realised that only the best possible image for France could result. The *Normandie* succeeded in all of the three intentions and even went beyond, such was her impact on the world in terms of decor, fashion, films, even children's toys—a fact that could not have been fully appreciated by the French at the outset.

Her keel plates were laid down in January 1931, at the Penhoët yards of St Nazaire, the birthplace of all the earlier great French liners. In the months that followed, alluring details regarding the new ship's statistics and accommodation were released tantalisingly with staggered frequency from the Paris home office. The same office was overwhelmed with suggestions for names—from *La Belle France* to *Président Paul Doumer*, the then recently assassinated President of France. Even *Maurice Chevalier* was placed among the candidates, no matter how serious the suggestion. At the same time, the shipyard crews of Clydebank, Scotland were busy at work on Britain's new national flagship and wonder liner. Something of a race had begun. However, despite the public's great interest and fascination in the new French liner and the lavish detail given to each aspect of her creation, the world-wide Depression was well under way together with unemployment and food queues. Consequently not all Frenchmen were flushed with pride when thinking of this extravagant new liner and its cost. To some, it was inexcuseable foolishness. She was after all being designed to impress and attract American passengers and, to some degree more specifically, the world's remaining millionaire class.

Madame Lebrun, the First Lady of France, named the ship *Normandie* during the launch ceremonies on October 29 1932. The unfinished 28,000-ton hull slipped into the Loire with a backwash that swept over 100 workers and visitors into the water. Immediately, she was linked with a high sense of the dramatic. John Maxtone Graham in his superb *The Only Way To Cross* quoted Ludwig Bemelmans as writing: 'She leaned to excesses . . . there was something of the fatal woman.'

Just as with the *Queen Mary*, construction work on the *Normandie* was temporarily stopped during the harshest of the Depression years. When labour

resumed, it was announced that the maiden voyage was postponed until the spring of 1935. She finally crossed in May of that year and immediately captured the Blue Riband with a run of 29.98 knots. The *Rex*'s two-year old record was 28.92. The *Normandie* instantly became headline news.

The interested public marvelled at her raked silhouette of three mighty red-and-black funnels, each of which diminished in height moving aft and the third of which was a dummy, merely a ventilator. Her outdoor, upper decks were meticulously cleared: not a ventilator or deckhouse or chain locker out of place. All these technical needs were hidden, with great care, below decks. The bow was exquisitely raked and displayed more clearly than ever that design certainly affected speed and performance, as testified on the maiden voyage. But if her overall appearance was striking, the interiors were the masterpiece.

The *Normandie* was certainly the most extravagantly decorated liner of her day, possibly of all time. The main dining room was done in hammered glass and bronze with glistening Lalique fixtures. It was slightly longer than the Hall of Mirrors at Versailles, rose three decks in height, and seated 1,000 guests. The theatre was the first ever fitted to a liner and included a stage for live performances. The indoor pool was 80 feet long of graduating levels, in consideration of the younger and more timid passengers. The Winter Garden included exotic birds in cages and sprays of water, certainly with an atmosphere far removed from that of the North Atlantic. The main lounge was covered with Dupas glass panels and special Aubusson tapestries were used to upholster the chairs. Each adjoining First-Class cabin was done in a totally different decor, resulting in 400 different concepts overall. Two de luxe apartments headed the First-Class section and these were located on the sun deck, tucked away from all other accommodation. Each had a private terrace, four bedrooms, a living room, servants' quarters and a dining room with individual serving pantry (below, there was a special dining room simply for travelling servants). Visitors to the *Normandie* were almost always impressed with her elegance, high quality, and spaciousness.

However, the excitement and acclaim were tainted by two worries: vibrations which plagued the great new French liner and the brand new British queen which was still being built across the Channel. Newly designed propellers eventually alleviated the former problem to some extent, but Cunard's liner was a nagging threat. When it was revealed that she would be at least 80,000 tons in size, it was evident that the *Normandie* would be displaced to the position of second largest with her 79,000 tons. Consequently, in the winter overhaul of 1935-6, just months before the new *Queen Mary*'s maiden trip, the French built a large deckhouse on one of the *Normandie*'s aft decks. Her tonnage was increased suddenly to 82,799, then 83,423. The *Mary* arrived finally with a figure of 80,774. The first battle was over: the French had won.

A more serious problem was that of the Blue Riband for which the *Queen Mary* was a challenger. Nearly three months after her maiden crossing, the British took the Riband in August 1936, at 30.14 knots. The *Normandie* regained the honours in the following March, with a recorded speed of 30.9 knots and then a further improvement of 31.2 knots in August 1937. The rivalry ended in August 1938, when the *Queen Mary* proved the fastest, at 31.6 knots. That record held until the *United States* appeared in 1952.

On August 28 1939 the *Normandie* was 'temporarily' laid up at New York's Pier 88, due to the threat of war in Europe. She was never to sail again. As the war machine advanced and, subsequently, with the fall of France herself, keeping the liner in the safety of still-neutral American waters seemed the most sensible course of action. The *Normandie* lay idle, her funnels capped, her furnishings overlaid with dust covers. and her staff reduced to 115.

While most of the world's large liners had begun trooping, speculation surrounded the *Normandie*. Would she eventually be used as a troop ship? And for whom? Would she be converted to an aircraft-carrier? This latter theory included sketches detailing how her innards could be dismantled and made into vast storage areas for aircraft. Her 1,028-foot hull could support an enormous flight deck. However, the troop-transport concept was the most appropriate and least costly. Five days after the attack on Pearl Harbor, on December 12 1941, the *Normandie* was officially seized by the United States government. On December 27, after being transferred to the command of the Navy Department, she was renamed USS *Lafayette* and conversion was begun at the pierside with crews from a local shipyard. Those luxurious interiors had to be stripped and taken ashore. An incredible sense of urgency echoed over the entire project. Officially, the former *Normandie* was listed as the Navy's transport *AP-53* and, after some dry-docking in Boston in mid-February, she was to begin work as the second-largest troop ship afloat (only the *Queen Elizabeth* was larger).

Then, mercilessly, on February 9, just days before estimated completion, sparks from a workmen's acetylene torch ignited a pile of kapok life jackets. Fire spread quickly on that bitterly cold mid-winter afternoon. Workers evacuated the ship and fire-fighting units both ashore and afloat arrived at the scene. Suddenly a covering of orange-brown smoke hung over New York. The excitement led to misjudgement: while the fire created considerable damage, the fire-fighters were overzealous and poured tons of water onto the smouldering ship. In the early hours of the next day, unable to withstand the additional pressure, she capsized and was lost.

On her side, the former *Normandie* presented the most difficult salvage job ever. Her funnels, masts, and superstructure had to be slowly and systematically removed by floating cranes as great pumps simultaneously pushed harbour water out of the vast, burnt-out hulk. This extraordinary operation was completed in the late summer of 1943, when she was righted amidst more talk that she would definitely now become an aircraft-carrier. The salvagers returned the vessel to the Navy Department on October 27, and within a week, she was towed to Brooklyn and laid up, pending further decision as to her future. Another two years passed. With the war now over, she was stricken from the Navy's list of ships on October 11 1945. Her original designer presented a scheme as to how she could be cut down and revitalised as a medium-sized passenger ship. The United States Maritime Commission, who now had title, had no interest or further use for the ship. She was sold to Lipsett Incorporated, a local scrap-metal firm, on October 3 1946, and grotesquely towed across New York Bay to Port Newark, New Jersey, for dismantling. This $60,000,000 ship of genius realised a pathetic $161,000 in the end. Within twelve months, only the legend remained.

Gross tonnage: 79,280 (1935), 82,799, then 83,423 (1936)
Length overall: 1,028 feet
Width: 117 feet
Machinery: Steam turbo-electric engines geared to quadruple screw
Speed: 29 knots
Capacity: 848 First, 670 Tourist, 454 Third
Built: Chantiers de l'Atlantique, St Nazaire, France, 1935
Demise: Burned and capsized in New York, February 9-10 1942; scrapped in 1946-7

Right *Maiden arrival in New York May 1935, after capturing the Blue Riband.*
See it flying at the main mast.
Below *A night-time shot at New York's Pier 88.*

Fifty Famous Liners

Normandie

Right *Burning—on that cold afternoon in February 1942.*

Left *A dramatic photo portraying the great size of the French flagship.*

Right *The* Normandie *on her side, like some beached whale.*

Normandie

Batory

The Polish Transatlantic Shipping Company was organised in 1930 and symbolised the Polish government's intention to operate a regular North-Atlantic passenger service. The government further intended to develop the seaport of Gdynia which, after World War 1, grew from a mere fishing village. The government's financial assistance permitted the acquisition of the Danish-flag Baltic American Line and its three passenger steamers, the 7,800-ton *Polonia* and the 6,500-ton sisters *Estonia* and *Lituania.* Thus, the new Polish service began almost immediately.

The trade was based on Gdynia and stopped at Copenhagen and Halifax before turning round in New York. Its mainstay was immigrants and within four years the success prompted a decision to build newer, larger ships. The Polish government entered into a trade agreement with the government of Italy, which provided that the Italians would build two 14,300-ton passenger ships in return for a series of coal shipments from Poland. The decision was a practical approach, particularly as both nations were still affected by the bitter Depression. Simultaneously, the company was retitled the Gdynia America Line.

The new twin sisters were built by the Cantieri Riuniti dell' Adriatico Shipyard in Monfalcone. They were powered by two Sulzer diesels, which rendered a service speed of 18 knots, and measured 526 feet in length, surely being the largest Polish ships ever built. Passenger accommodation was designed to cater for 370 Tourist Class and 400 Third Class (the tourist section being equivalent to standard Cabin Class of the period).

The first to be finished, the *Pilsudski*, sailed from Italy for Gdynia during the summer of 1935 and shortly thereafter entered service to New York. The second ship, christened *Batory* in honour of the sixteenth-century Polish king, Stephen Batory, crossed on her maiden run in May of 1936. Both ships were highly successful and were so designed as to trade to the Caribbean during the winter off-season.

In September 1939, following the invasion and fall of Poland, the *Pilsudski* was transferred to the British and outfitted as an armed merchant cruiser. Unfortunately, her military career was quite brief. On November 26 she was torpedoed and sunk by an enemy submarine outside the River Humber.

The *Batory* fared more fortunately. She remained in American waters in the fall of 1939 following a mutiny by her crew members and was laid up in the Hudson River, off Yonkers, New York. A year or so later, she was designated as a troop ship under the Allied Command and began sailing to ports around the globe, a role which lasted until 1946. Upon return to the Gdynia America Line, she was refitted in Antwerp and reappeared in peace-time on the Atlantic, in April 1947. She sailed single-handed between Gdynia, Copenhagen, and New York with First and Tourist-Class accommodation.

Commencing in May 1949 and lasting through January 1951, the *Batory* was the topic of a series of tense political incidents. American labour resented her supposed Communist ownership, particularly in a time of 'Cold War'. Furthermore, an accused spy escaped from New York aboard the liner. Stevedores flatly refused to handle the ship and her service was suspended.

The *Batory* was dry-docked and extensively overhauled in Hebburn-on-Tyne, England. Her accommodation was improved and she was repainted with a tropical dove-grey hull. The Gdynia America Line title was dropped in favour of the more inter-national-sounding Polish Ocean Lines. In August 1951, she was despatched on a new service: sailing from Gdynia and Southampton for Gibraltar, Malta, Aden, Karachi, and Bombay.

156

Within the following years, the Polish Ocean Lines made apparent their interest in returning to the North Atlantic. In early 1957, the *Batory* was sent to Bremerhaven for thorough rebuilding and alterations. The ship's eight public rooms were rearranged and redecorated and the 12 lifeboats raised off the decks to create further open spaces. The accommodation was restyled in more transatlantic fashion, with a mere 76 First-Class berths and as many as 740 in Tourist Class.

The *Batory* first sailed from Gdynia for Copenhagen, Southampton, and Montreal on August 26 1957. Thereafter, sailings were run on a ten-month period (March to December) each year and included occasional calls in London (instead of Southampton), Le Havre, Bremerhaven, Helsinki, and Quebec City (instead of Montreal). In subsequent years, there were also a number of winter sailings to Boston. Furthermore, she sailed as a 500-passenger single-class cruise ship during the deep winter months, on holiday runs from either London or Southampton to the Canaries, West Africa, Portugal, and the Caribbean.

The *Batory* was a great success on the Canadian–North Atlantic run despite the intensity of competition from the air which other lines were facing, especially during the 1960s. The greater portion of her passengers were Polish nationals and the majority of older passengers were 'ship-minded' (as opposed to air enthusiasts). Also, no direct air services had developed between Canada and Poland, and so the *Batory* was in demand.

In view of the great success which the Polish Ocean Lines met on returning to the Atlantic, serious consideration was given in the early and mid-1960s to the construction of a 20,000-ton liner as a replacement for the *Batory* and which was rumoured to be named *Polonia*. However, in the end, high labour and shipbuilding costs ruled out the possibility and the 15,000-ton *Maasdam* was acquired from Holland-America Line instead. She was completely refitted in Gdynia, rechristened *Stefan Batory*, and introduced on the Montreal run in April 1969.

The *Batory*, which by this time had reached the age of 33, completed her final sailing to Canada in December 1968. Thereafter, she did some cruising to the Canaries and Caribbean before being formally decommissioned. The Polish government—as owner of the ship—decided that she should remain under the national flag. Consequently, for the price of one zloty (24 being equivalent to one American dollar), the *Batory* was sold to the Municipality of Gdynia for use as a floating hotel and accommodation centre. This phase lasted for two years, until the spring of 1971, when she was sold to Hong Kong ship-breakers.

Gross tonnage: 14,287
Length overall: 526 feet
Width: 71 feet
Draft: 24 feet
Machinery: Sulzer diesels geared to twin screw
Speed: 18 knots
Capacity: 370 Tourist, 400 Third (1936); 76 First, 740 Tourist (1957)
Built: Cantieri Riuniti dell'Adriatico, Trieste, Italy, 1936
Demise: Scrapped in Hong Kong, 1971

At the shipyard at Monfalcone, the Batory *prepares for her first sea-trials.*

Above *The maiden arrival in New York in May 1936, with numerous harbour excursion craft in the background including the* Commonwealth *and the* City of Keansburg.

Left *While in dry dock, the bow appears lofty and sleek.*

Right *In need of some repairs, she is put into Todd Ship-yards in Weehawken, New York harbour.*

Batory

Queen Mary

As the renewed age of the superliner began in the late 1920s with Germany's *Bremen* and *Europa*, British companies were not to be left out. Canadian Pacific ordered their biggest ever, the 42,000-ton *Empress of Britain*. White Star Line signed with Harland & Wolff at Belfast for a 60,000 tonner, intended to be called *Oceanic*. The latter's proposed running-mate was to be in the form of a third giant: Cunard's 75,000-ton flagship, still unnamed but thought to be called *Victoria*. It seemed a sparkling era. Then, the hideousness of the worldwide Depression changed the best-intended plans. While in the earliest stages of construction, White Star's *Oceanic* had to be abandoned and her steel found its way into a more economical ship, the 27,000-ton *Britannic*. As the *Empress* neared completion, only the Cunarder remained.

John Brown & Company had been selected as the building firm and the first plates were laid down two days after Christmas, 1930. The design plans showed not only a large ship (the world's largest at the best estimations) but a very powerful one capable of making the Atlantic passage in four days or even less. Could Cunard be considering the Blue Riband again, after the *Mauretania*'s loss to the *Bremen* in 1929? The answer from the Liverpool head office was and continued to be 'no'.

Almost amazingly, Cunard had not built a major passenger liner since the *Aquitania* of 1914. Her blueprints were, in fact, used in preparations for this new supership and helped to support a design concept favoured by Cunard directors that Atlantic liners should appear sturdy, dependable, and reliable. Cunard did not share the modernistic approach used by the French Line, for example, in planning its new record-breaker. The new Cunarder would look solid, traditional, and generally unpretentious.

The havoc of the Depression reached Clydebank by December 1931, a full year after construction had begun. The building was halted and all but a handful of workers were laid off. The great hull sat—silent, lonesome, and guarded by a small maintenance gang. Debates took place in London as to whether the British government should advance Cunard the monies needed to continue construction. Some thought the ship was wasteful, intended for the 'bygone' millionaire class of America. Fortunately, the proposal to extend a loan was approved and, after over two years, building was resumed on April 3 1934. Had it not been for this halt, the Cunarder would have been in service before her rival, the French *Normandie*, then still being built across the Channel in St Nazaire. As it was, the French completed their ship earlier and therefore had the first to exceed 1,000 feet, the first over 60,000 tons, and—far worse—captured the Blue Riband. The Cunarder could only hope to have her day of glory somewhat later.

Her Majesty Queen Mary consented to launch and name the new liner, which would be the first time a merchant ship was so honoured by a reigning British monarch. In the months just prior to the launch, members of Cunard and the Royal Household met to discuss the choice of names. Rumour was that it would be the *Victoria*. A tale of the day (and one that still persists) is that the Cunard Chairman called on King George V at Buckingham Palace and requested permission to name the ship 'after England's most illustrious queen'. George V supposedly misunderstood and, not even thinking of his grandmother, announced that his wife would be delighted! His wife was, of course, Mary of Teck, Queen Consort. Another theory is that Cunard intended from the very beginning to call their new ship the *Queen Mary*, no matter how secret the decision. The firm had just merged with the White Star Line and as something of a compromise for this totally new, unmatched liner, reconciling that company's 'ic' nomenclature with Cunard's 'ia' naming policy (after Roman provinces), the royal selection seemed a good choice. Furthermore, 1935 was Silver Jubilee Year and what better way to help celebrate than to name Britain's greatest liner yet built after the existing monarch?

In any event, the public first learned of the name choice on September 26 1934, when the King and Queen travelled to the John Brown yards for the launching. The Queen used a bottle of Australian wine for the naming ceremony and recorded in her diary, later that same day: 'A most impressive sight but unfortunately it rained all day.' The *Queen Mary* moved to a fitting-out pier.

Queen Mary herself and other members of the Royal Family went to Southampton in May 1936, to inspect the finished liner. On the 27th of that month, Cunard's new ship sailed for New York. Facts and figures released in the Press amazed the interested public. The 140-ton rudder had a door in its side so that it could be inspected internally in dry dock. There were 16-ton anchors, each with 990 feet of anchor chain. There were 151 watertight compartments, 10,000,000 rivets, 2,000 portholes and windows, 2,500 square feet of glass, and 257,000 turbine blades. The three whistles weighed one ton each and could be heard for ten miles. There were 700 clocks and 600 telephones on board. One report described Cunard's growth as the leading transatlantic company, from an entire fleet totalling 81,126 tons in 1876 to one in which a single ship weighed 81,000 tons a century later.

The *Queen Mary* excelled. She made worldwide headlines. She captured the Blue Riband from the *Normandie* in August 1936, with a run of 30.63 knots during a westbound crossing. The Riband went back to the French ship in March 1937, then only to be regained permanently by the British liner in August 1938, with a recorded 31.6 knots. The *Queen Mary* was the world's fastest liner until the arrival in 1952 of the *United States*. She was also the only ship of the 1930s super-class to show a profit for her owners. Cunard wisely decided to build a running-mate, which would appear in 1940 as the *Queen Elizabeth*. Although the *Queen Mary* lacked the glitter and fascination that surrounded the *Normandie*, she was a very successful ship that more than pleased her owners. It seems the only concern was her rolling at sea. A crewman once said that 'she could roll the milk out of a cup of tea.'

Along with the *Normandie*, the *Ile de France*, and the second *Mauretania*, the *Queen Mary* was laid up in New York in September 1939, supposedly awaiting an end to the political crisis in Europe. The end was far away. She was repainted in grey and then briefly, in early March of the next year, sat across Pier 90 from her brand new counterpart, the *Queen Elizabeth*. The *Mary* quietly left for Sydney later that same month and was outfitted for trooping. The *Elizabeth* followed in November.

At first, both 'Queens' operated across the Indian Ocean with troops for Africa from Australia, returning with the wounded, the evacuees, and the prisoners of the war. The *Mary* returned to the Atlantic in 1942, and began something of a shuttle service to Gourock, Scotland, from New York. She averaged 15,000 service personnel per crossing and because of her great speed was beyond the scope of any sort of available escort craft. Consequently, she sailed alone, at top speed, and in a zig-zag fashion on courses that were never repeated from voyage to voyage. Hitler was envious and offered the Iron Cross and a $250,000 reward to the U-boat Commander who could sink her. With great fortune the 'Queen' escaped. However, one very sad occasion tarnished her otherwise brilliant war record. On October 2 1942, at top speed, off the Irish Coast, she rammed and sliced in half the HMS *Curacoa*, an escort cruiser. The warship sank within three minutes and all but 26 of her 364 crew members were lost. Because of the danger of possible undetected U-boats, the *Mary* could not stop to rescue any survivors and was forced to continue at top speed.

The *Elizabeth* joined the transatlantic military run in 1943 and for the next two years the two 'Queens' maintained a weekly service, ferrying thousands of military passengers. The *Mary* established the record for the greatest number of souls carried in a single ship, in July 1943, with 16,683 on board. Quite rightly, Winston Churchill said that the two 'Queens' helped to win the war in Europe by at least a year.

The *Mary* was decommissioned finally, in September 1946, and sent to the John Brown yards for refitting. On July 31 of the following year, she resumed service between Southampton and New York and for the first time was joined commercially by the *Elizabeth*. The two-ship team, making a weekly departure in each direction, was the first in history and created the most economically successful pair of ships ever built. For the next 15 years or so, the *Queen Mary* and *Queen Elizabeth* (the former always being the slightly more popular) were superbly profitable to Cunard.

Cunard thought of a three-class replacement for the *Mary* in the early 1960s that was affectionately dubbed the *Q3*. It never came to pass. Designs were reworked with considerable thought given to cruising and the result was the *Q4* or *Queen Elizabeth 2*, as she was named. During the 1960s, the *Mary*'s passenger figures began to decline, as a result of the rising jet aircraft age and Cunard's propensity for sending the ship across the Atlantic in the bleakest months of winter. Occasionally she went cruising. Her first such trip was in December 1963, on a week's run from Southampton to Las Palmas and back. Later, there were holiday voyages from New York to Nassau and then a large-scale romp around the Mediterranean. She lacked central air-conditioning and vast swimming pool-lido decks so favoured by the cruise clientele sailing to the tropics. She could hardly be expected to be an outright success. By 1967, she showed a loss of £750,000 in her overall operations. Having no alternative, Cunard decided to retire both 'Queens'.

The *Mary* was the first to go, leaving New York with a gala farewell of escort craft in September 1967. Rumours circulated that she might become an Australian immigrant carrier or, worse still, a public high school for the City of New York. Finally, the City of Long Beach, California, far removed from any of the liner's movements yet rich from oil revenue and wanting a top-notch tourist attraction, secured the *Mary*—the last of the three-stack Atlantic liners—as the perfect gimmick, for just over $3,500,000

As the deal was completed, the liner left Southampton for the last time on October 31, with 1,040 passengers, on a nostalgic final cruise that was the most exhaustive of her entire career. She travelled for 39 days, touching at Lisbon, Las Palmas, Rio de Janeiro, Valparaiso, Callao, Balboa, Acapulco, and finally to her new home: Long Beach. She carried four London 'double-decker' buses on her aft decks, flew a 310-foot long (for 31 years service) 'paying off' pennant, and each of 800 crew members received a farewell bonus of £40. After 1,001 crossings, she would never sail again.

She opened as a museum-hotel-convention centre on May 10 1971 to mixed reviews. Some were horrified to see souvenir stands lining the sun and promenade decks; others were thankful that she was being preserved. The restoration cost a shocking $72,000,000, yet the city was encouraged by the 1.4 million visitors who came aboard in the first year. However, by 1976, this had declined to 450,000 and by December 1978, there were strong rumours circulating that she was for sale, even for scrapping. At the time of writing, the *Queen Mary*'s existence is in question, but one can only be pleased that, as one of the greatest of the Atlantic's grand liners, she continues to survive.

Gross tonnage: 80,774 (1936), 81,235 (1937), 81,237 (1947)
Length overall: 1,018 feet
Width: 118 feet
Machinery: Steam turbines geared to quadruple screw
Speed: 29 knots
Capacity: 776 Cabin, 784 Tourist, 579 Third (1936); 711 First, 707 Cabin, 577 Tourist (1947)
Built: John Brown & Company Limited, Clydebank, Scotland, 1930–6

Fifty Famous Liners

Above *The* Queen Mary *arriving in Southampton on March 27 1936, to be dry docked, she passes the flag-bedecked* Majestic *and* Windsor Castle.

Below *A month and a day later, she leaves for her trials, passing the* Berengaria.

Above *All grey, she steams into New York harbour during her trooping days and is saluted by the ferry* Wilkes-Barre *(note white puff of steam from the ferry's stack).*
Left *The main dining saloon of the* Queen Mary.
Below *In New York between the* Mauretania *(below) and the* Britannic, *with the sleek little Furness liner* Fort Townsend *at the top.*

An artist's conception of the Queen Mary *in Trafalgar Square.*

Nieuw Amsterdam

Probably of all the Dutch liners the *Nieuw Amsterdam* was the most favoured. She was built as Holland's 'ship of state'—the biggest yet in the homeland and a tour de force in terms of design and decoration. Although created in the midst of the world Depression, she was bestowed with two rather positive nicknames: 'the ship of peace' and 'the ship of tomorrow'. Regarding the former, she was built without a single military ingredient, this despite the threatening political situation in Europe, particularly in Germany. As to the second title, her decor was highlighted by some quite modern approaches, some of which were inspired by the Paris World's Fair of 1933 and others that would later be used in the 1939 Fair in New York.

The Holland-America Line had some financial reserves in addition to a Dutch government loan that allowed for serious thoughts on the subject of a new national flagship in the middle 1930s. Her name was to be *Prinsendam* and she was to be built at the Rotterdam Dry Dock Company yards in her home port. Unlike the 28,000-ton *Statendam* of 1929, which was highly traditional with its three thin funnels, the new ship would be much more sleek and use a balanced design consisting of two well-proportioned funnels against two tall masts. Her overall silhouette came to be, in fact, one of the most pleasing of the 1930s generation of passenger liners.

The launching took place on April 10 1937. The name by this time had been changed to *Nieuw Amsterdam*, honouring the tiny Dutch settlement in North America that became New York City. Her Majesty Queen Wilhelmina officiated at the ceremony in full view of thousands of guests, workers, and their families. Special precautions had to be taken as the liner slid along the building ways and slipped into the narrow River Maas. Ten large braces were welded into the hull and consequently, as the ship was launched, huge chains that were connected to these braces were released two at a time. The weight of these chains stopped the *Nieuw Amsterdam* within her own 758-foot length just as she was completely waterborne.

After fitting-out, the new flagship sailed to New York from Rotterdam, via Boulogne and Southampton, on May 10 1938. She won great praise

instantly. Although not of the superliner class, she was generally acknowledged to be one of the most extraordinarily beautiful ships of her day. In the following 17½ return voyages, the *Nieuw Amsterdam* established herself as one of the best money-making passenger vessels in the world. Then, for Holland's 'ship of peace', the situation changed.

When the war began in the autumn of 1939, the *Nieuw Amsterdam* was laid up for safety reasons at her Hoboken pier, just across from the skyscrapers of Manhattan. In the following spring, she was pressed into cruise service, sailing out of New York to ports like Bermuda and Kingston and Havana. When the Nazi invasion of Holland began on May 10, the *Nieuw Amsterdam* hurriedly returned to her American home port to take up a far more serious role: that of military troop ship. She was taken over by the British Ministry of Transport, on behalf of the exiled Dutch government, and dry-docked, first at Brooklyn, then at Halifax. Her war-time role had begun. Within the next six years, she carried 378,361 personnel on voyages that amounted to 530,452 miles (or the equivalent to 21 times around the world). These figures represent the astonishing averages of 8,599 persons on each of the 44 voyages of 12,056 miles apiece!

The luxurious interiors were removed in Singapore, later in 1940, and there, due to the haste and carelessness of war, the fine carpets and beautiful wooden tables and chairs were left lying on the pier-side. They were exposed to all kinds of weather before finally being shipped to Australia and then San Francisco for safe-keeping. On board, the Grand Hall had been converted to a duplex dormitory that slept 600 servicemen in three tiers. The theatre held an additional 386, while there were 22 officers in each of the original de luxe cabins and 18 in the former First-Class doubles.

The *Nieuw Amsterdam*'s routing was exceptionally diverse, touching at such ports as Cape Town, Mombasa, Bombay, Aden, Sydney, Wellington, Surabaya, San Francisco, Boston, and Liverpool. In July 1941, she was selected to transport the entire Greek Royal Family into war-time exile, from Port Suez to Durban. In May 1944, while the ship was berthed at Hoboken, Her Royal

Highness Princess Juliana, daughter of Queen Wilhelmina, came aboard for a small buffet lunch and a tour of the liner. The Dutch crew members were deeply inspired by the royal visit.

Emotions ran high on April 10 1946 as the *Nieuw Amsterdam*—or as one spectator commented 'the darling of the Dutch'—returned to her home port. She steamed into Rotterdam harbour surrounded by every possible floating object, dressed in flags, sounding her horns, and with her stacks specially repainted in Holland-America's green, yellow, and white colours despite her otherwise drab military-grey livery. It was exactly the ninth anniversary of her launch and to the Dutch on this day she was symbolic of true liberation.

It took 12 weeks to remove the war-time fittings before the actual reconversion for luxury service could begin. The process was stupendous, particularly in a post-war Europe that was short of both skilled manpower and materials. The entire wiring system on board was replaced as was all the brass work. Some 12,000 square feet of glass had to be renewed, 2,700 square feet of teak making up the outdoor decks and all the handrails had to be scraped free of thousands of initials left by the service personnel. Furthermore, 500 tables were restored and 3,000 chairs re-upholstered, and all the 374 bathrooms rebuilt with new fixtures. Fourteen months later, in October 1947, the *Nieuw Amsterdam* was ready to return to commercial operation on the North Atlantic.

Her ability to build long lists of loyal passengers was just as it had been in those brief pre-war years. She was again a great favourite. Holland-America more than recovered their investment in her. Yet, most surprising, though there was talk of a sister ship, nothing came to pass until as late as 1956 when designs were drawn up for the 38,000-ton *Rotterdam* which was to be the new Dutch flagship.

Completed three years later, in the summer of 1959, the *Rotterdam* was a fine liner, the first on the Atlantic run to dispense with the customary funnel and instead use twin uptakes aft, built with an eye to considerable off-season cruising, and a stark affirmation on the part of her owners of their confidence in the future of passenger shipping despite the growing strength and popularity of jet aircraft. However, the *Nieuw Amsterdam* retained the greater reverence. Her sense of character and charm could not be diminished even against her more-than-twenty years of age. These facts, together with the ship's historical role began to inspire an even greater affection among the Dutch themselves.

Two refits ensured the *Nieuw Amsterdam*'s contemporary status. In 1957, she was given full air-conditioning and some improvements to her accommodation. Four years later, she was converted to a two-class liner with berthing arrangements that could be adapted to the trade requirements. According to booking demand, her capacity could read 691 First and 583 Tourist Class or 301 First and 972 Tourist. In the peak season months from April to October, Holland-America offered service on what it called 'the Big Three'—the *Rotterdam*, the *Nieuw Amsterdam*, and the 24,000-ton *Statendam*, which had been added in 1957. The ships sailed from New York every Friday at noon for Southampton, Le Havre, and Rotterdam and thereby created an arrangement that was useful to hundreds of thousands of passengers at the time.

When the rivalry of the jet could no longer be ignored, the *Statendam* was shifted to year-round cruising from California. The transatlantic liner trade was approaching its twilight. Holland-America ships began to spend more time on tropical cruises and then only the *Nieuw Amsterdam* remained steadfast on the trade out of Rotterdam. However, there were some frightening moments in August 1967 when she had a severe mechanical breakdown. Her anxiously waiting passengers had to be ferried across the Channel and put aboard the *United States* and Cunard's *Caronia*. The future of the *Nieuw Amsterdam* was seriously threatened. Could Holland's beloved liner be sold for scrapping? Was she seriously beyond economic repair? Rumours, heightened by newspaper reports, hinted that she was finished. But after some extensive deliberation, Holland-America directors fortunately decided that she could be saved and would see several more years of financial usefulness. She was taken to the Dutch shipyards of Wilton-Fijenoord in Schiedam, had a huge opening cut in her starboard side and was fitted with new boilers. The *Nieuw Amsterdam* would survive.

By the late 1960s, she worked single-handedly on the Atlantic and, in fact, became the last Holland-America transatlantic liner. By the end of 1971, with summer passenger figures continuing to plunge and operating expenses increasing, she was assigned to permanent cruising from American ports to the Caribbean. Along with North German Lloyd, United States Lines, and others soon to follow, the Holland-America Line ended its long tradition of port-to-port Atlantic service. The company terminal at Rotterdam would be used thereafter only by visiting cruise ships.

As operational costs continued to rise, the *Nieuw Amsterdam*'s Dutch crew was reduced greatly and replaced by Indonesians, supposedly saving the Line several millions of dollars each year. Her home port was changed to Willemstad, Curaçao, in the Dutch West Indies, an act prompted by high taxes in Holland itself. Problems mounted. During 1973, Holland-America showed a loss of $12.5 million, prodded by sky-rocketing fuel costs and labour rates. A stiff tightening in the operations of the company was in order and the *Nieuw Amsterdam* was the prime target, largely due to her age and vast fuel consumption. Within months, by December 1973, she was sold for scrapping. There were, of course, a flood of rumours and emotional cries to save her, the most prominent suggestion being to return the liner to Holland for use as a combination museum-hotel similar to the fate of the *Queen Mary* in California but again, costs were prohibitive.

She left Port Everglades, passed through the Panama Canal, stopped at Los Angeles for fuel and further provisions and then proceeded across the Pacific at an almost deliberately slow pace. By March, she had reached Kaohsiung, Taiwan, and the inevitable was at hand. By the end of the year, she was gone.

Gross tonnage: 36,287 (1938), 36,667 (1947), 36,982 (1961)
Length overall: 758 feet
Width: 88 feet
Draft: 30 feet
Machinery: Steam turbines geared to twin screw
Speed: 20.5 knots
Capacity: 556 First, 455 Tourist, 209 Third (1938); 552 First, 426 Cabin, 209 Tourist (1947); adjustable from 691 First and 583 Tourist to 301 First and 972 Tourist (1961)
Built: Rotterdam Dry Dock Company, Rotterdam, the Netherlands, 1938
Demise: Scrapped in Kaohsiung, Taiwan, 1974

Above *Maiden arrival in New York's Lower Bay, May 1938.*
Left *It was calculated that the* Nieuw Amsterdam *was 425 times larger than Henry Hudson's sailing ship,* Half Moon.
Below *Later in her life, in the 1960s, she had a grey hull with a slim yellow band.*

The impressive bow of the Nieuw Amsterdam *looms ahead as she prepares to dock at Hòboken.*
She is coming in without tugs during a strike.

Fifty Famous Liners

Oranje

The year 1939 was in vast contrast to the earlier days of the 1930s which had been hard hit by the Great Depression, when steamship owners were forced to lay up, sell, and even scrap some of their passenger ships. Instead, that last year of the decade was something of a renaissance for the liner trade, even despite the bitter war clouds that were forming in Europe and the Far East. The British, French, Americans, and even the Germans and Japanese had an impressive output of passenger-type ships for trade routes throughout the world. The Dutch—a substantial merchant shipping power and hardly to be outdone—had just finished their biggest liner to date, the 36,000-ton *Nieuw Amsterdam*, when attention turned to the Nederland Line and their plans for a fast new flagship for the colonial trade to Batavia.

Her Majesty Queen Wilhelmina travelled to the Netherlands Shipbuilding Company yard in Amsterdam, on September 8 1938, for the naming and launch ceremonies. The name *Oranje* was chosen in tribute to the Dutch Royal Family and therefore the occasion had the Queen's special interest. She quite happily smashed the bottle of champagne across the bow of the new ship and expected the hull to begin sliding down the ways. To the horror of her owners and the shipyard crews, and the amazement of the other assembled guests, the 656-foot long liner failed to free itself and remained tightly in the building slip. When the Queen and the guests departed, the *Oranje* was still high above the water. Workmen brought in hydraulic rams and on that same evening, almost unnoticed, the new flagship allowed herself to slide gently into the harbour waters.

Accommodation was designed for 717 passengers in four classes: First, Second, Third, and Fourth. Her exterior with its single mast and stack was far more modern than other Nederland liners but the interiors reflected the colonial service for which she was designed. For example, in First Class, there was a 'Cane Lounge', done in bamboo, with exotic potted palms and overhead fans. She took as her maiden voyage a cruise from Amsterdam to Madeira and back in August 1939, and then left for Batavia via Suez on September 4.

The war was quick to interrupt her schedules and, in December, she was laid up in Surabaya for temporary safety. Over a year passed before, in February 1941, she was moved to Sydney and fitted out as a hospital ship for the Royal Australian Navy, although still under the Dutch flag. She was formally commissioned on July 30 to a service that would last five years.

The *Oranje* was given high praise for her role in the war effort when she was returned to her owners by the Australians on July 19 1946. The Dutch lines were in a serious state of shortages, complicated heavily by their severe war losses, and it was therefore decided to delay any major refit for the flagship. She was quickly returned instead to the Amsterdam/Batavia service with her major overhaul being done in stages until finally completed in 1949.

She was transferred to a new around-the-world service in February 1950, that still included the Dutch East Indies but also called at Australia, Singapore, and Panama. She sailed outbound in a westerly pattern and returned to Holland via the Mediterranean. There were occasional spells of

cruising, such as her first post-war trip to Madeira and Lisbon in June 1951.

As competition rose in the late 1950s, the *Oranje* was part of the three-liner plan (the others being the *Willem Ruys* and *Johan van Oldenbarnevelt*) that merged the once-rival Nederland and Royal Rotterdam Lloyd Lines into a joint around-the-world service, and that included a major refit for the ship in Amsterdam. Her passenger spaces were rearranged to more modern standards, with 323 in First Class and 626 in Tourist. She continued to gain high praise and was particularly noteworthy for the excellence of her Singapore-Chinese catering staff. Cruises were also part of her new schedule, including a 21-day jaunt from Amsterdam to the Mediterranean in 1960 for which minimum fares were £170 in First Class and £110 in Tourist.

One of *Oranje*'s greatest honours came in May 1962, when she was selected to make a special royal cruise for the silver wedding celebrations of the Queen of the Netherlands. Some 130 guests were gathered at the plush Amstel Hotel and then taken by limousines and special buses to the dockside in Amsterdam to board the ship. In addition to Queen Juliana, Prince Bernhard, Crown Princess Beatrix and other members of the Dutch Royal Family, Queen Elizabeth and Prince Philip, King Olav V of Norway, King Baudouin and Queen Fabiola of Belgium, Grand Duchess Charlotte of Luxembourg, Princess Marina of Kent, and the Shah and Empress of Iran were also passengers on the short cruise in the North Sea. The Dutch government paid $28,000 towards the affair with the remainder of the cost coming from the Queen herself.

Oranje's days were shortened, however, mostly by the intense competition from other lines also engaged in worldwide service. On September 4 1964, she was handed over to her new owners, Flotta Lauro of Naples, renamed *Angelina Lauro* and immediately set sail for an Italian shipyard. The result was one of Italy's most exhaustive rebuilding programmes—one that included a new flared bow, the reshaping of her entire superstructure, all new interior accommodation, a vast lido deck, and a tall winged funnel of the most modern design. The original *Oranje* was hardly recongisable. There was a set-back, however. On August 24–26 1965, she was seriously damaged by a fire at the yard and so bad was it that it resulted in the deaths of six workmen.

The *Angelina Lauro* was ready for her new career in March 1966, some 4,000 tons larger than before. The new accommodation was balanced between 189 in First Class, 1,050 in Tourist, and a further 377 interchangeable. Her new service was primarily an immigrant one, although her facilities were of an extremely high standard that included a vast amount of private cabin plumbing, tasteful Italian decor, and such additional features as closed-circuit television. Her trade routing was on the extensive northern Europe/Mediterranean/Australia circuit, one that included passage through Suez (and Panama on occasions), later re-routing via South Africa and with periodic return voyages by way of the Straits of Magellan and ports in South America.

When the Australian government's highly prized immigrant contract was given over to the Greek-flag Chandris Lines in 1970, the Lauro Line service weakened and rather quickly became unprofitable. The *Angelina Lauro* made her last 'line voyages' to Australia in 1972, and was thereafter assigned to permanent cruising, mostly from Florida to the Caribbean with about 800 passengers, all First Class. She went back to the Mediterranean for further cruising in 1976, and then only to begin a three-year charter to the Costa Line in April 1978 that brought her back to the Caribbean.

Just short of her fortieth birthday, on March 30 1979, she was swept by a fire that began in the galley and quickly engulfed the entire ship. Fortunately, her passengers were ashore on shopping expeditions in St Thomas, leaving only the crew, all of whom escaped without serious injury. As for the ship herself, she was quite finished. She settled on the harbour bottom with her upper decks leaning against the pier at a twenty-degree list. When the fire was finally extinguished on April 5, she was a charred wreck beyond any sort of economic hope. Rumours floated about that one Caribbean island wanted her for use as a fishing reef, another for a breakwater, but scrapping was the only realistic solution. Salvage began in May, with the Neptun Bergungsgesellschaft GmbH of Hamburg using a diving barge, pontoon, and floating crane.

During the refloating process, she was sold to Eckhardt & Company, also of Hamburg, for scrapping but was then promptly resold to Taiwanese buyers for the same purpose. She left St Thomas on July 30, under tow of the deep-sea tug *Nippon*

Maru. As they passed through the Panama Canal, the 26,300-ton tanker *Mara* was added to the tow for the long, very slow voyage to the Kaohsiung scrappers. When well into the Pacific, on September 21, the crew of the tug reported that the *Angelina Lauro* had developed a serious list. Little could be done. Two days later, the towline was cut and she slipped under. (It is rather ironic that less than two weeks later, on October 3, another passenger ship—the 9,000-ton *Bonaire Star*, ex-*Jerusalem*, ex-*Bahama Star*—also sank in the Pacific while under tow. She too was bound for the scrapyards of Taiwan.)

Gross tonnage: 20,017 (1939), 20,551 (1959), 24,377 (1966)
Length overall: 656 feet (1939), 672 feet (1966)
Width: 83 feet
Machinery: Sulzer-type diesels geared to triple screw
Speed: 21 knots (26 knots maximum)
Capacity: 717 passengers in four classes: First, Second, Third, Fourth (1939); 323 First, 626 Tourist (1959); 189 First, 377 interchangeable, 1,050 Tourist (1966); 800 First (1972)
Built: Netherlands Shipbuilding and Dry Dock Company, Amsterdam, the Netherlands, 1939
Demise: While under tow in the Pacific, sank on September 23 1979

The Oranje *in her Royal Dutch Mail colours. Note the fact that she has no mainmast aft.*

Left *She was fitted with considerable cargo space as well as an unusually high number of booms and derricks* (Courtesy of Roger Sherlock).

Below left *Thoroughly rebuilt as the* Angelina Lauro, *the ship was given a new funnel with a winged smoke-deflecting top* (Courtesy of the Vincent Messina Collection).

Right *Sketch by co-author Braynard who happened to be present aboard the* Oceanic *alongside while the* Angelina Lauro *was still smoking.*

From the rail of the OCEANIC's Sun Deck - leaving St. Thomas - April 2, 1979 - The turned out hulk of the ANGELINA LAURO of Costa Line

Below *She burns to death in St Thomas in March 1979* (Courtesy of Associated Press).

Andes

The completion of the 25,600-ton *Andes* in September 1939 was marked not simply as the completion of the Royal Mail Lines' largest passenger ship built to date, but signified the centenary of the firm itself. It had been exactly one hundred years since a Royal Charter had been granted to the company that became the Royal Mail Steam Packet Company. Consequently, the arrival of the new flagship, *Andes*, was more than just that of another new passenger liner. Yet, despite all the happy and elaborate planning, the outbreak of hostilities came a little more than three weeks prior to the new vessel's planned departure for South America.

She was launched on March 7 1939, by Viscountess Craigavon, the wife of the Prime Minister of Northern Ireland, at the Harland & Wolff yards in Belfast. Meticulous care had been taken in her design so that she would not only be Royal Mail's largest and fastest ship, but a sure competitor to the high standard French, Italian, and German liners already in service to the east coast of South America. Further thought had been given to periodic cruising for which she was fitted with a large bunker capacity.

Andes was still at the fitting-out dock when war was declared and her scheduled maiden sailing from Southampton, set for September 26, was cancelled. The supplies and deliveries of handsome new furnishings were set aside and re-routed, and her already freshly painted hull, superstructure, and great yellow funnel were redone in tones of grey. The festivities, the gala plans, and the capacity list of inaugural passengers suddenly seemed inappropriate. Instead, *Andes'* first voyage took her from England on December 9, to Halifax, and then back with the first load of Canadian troops brought to Britain for the war effort. From there, she set a course through the Mediterranean, passed through the Suez Canal, stopped in Colombo and Singapore, and finally reached Hong Kong—in an area of the world far removed from any of her original intentions and design. Quickly, she was ordered to Lyttleton and Wellington, and then despatched homeward again through the Indian Ocean. She was, during this trip, one of a large and mighty convoy that included the *Queen Mary*, the *Aquitania*, the *Mauretania*, the *Empress of Britain*, the *Empress of Japan*, and the *Empress of Canada*. Despite the sadness and urgency of the time, what a most incredible sight these seven liners must have been to passing ships. Altogether, there was a total of 19 funnels!

The following voyages for the *Andes* included a return trip to Iceland, and then a sailing to the Middle East via Cape Town with 3,000 servicemen aboard, that was so overcrowded that 500 of them slept on deck and so international that 13 different languages were spoken. Thereafter, her voyages were extremely diverse and included visits to ports throughout the world. However, it has been recorded that she featured in at least one more of the war's great convoys, this one including Cunard's *Georgic*, several P & O 'Strath' liners, an equal number of Canadian Pacific 'Empresses' and 'Duchesses', at least a pair of Orient Line 'O Boats', various 'Castles' from Union Castle, the French *Pasteur*, and the Dutch *Dempo* and *Johan van Oldenbarnevelt*.

One of the more glorious duties for *Andes* came in May 1945, when she was selected to carry the Norwegian government from its war-time exile in London back across the North Sea to a triumphant reception in Oslo. Aircraft flew overhead, dozens of small craft created an escort, and thousands lined the waterfront as she steamed, flag-bedecked and sounding her horns, to a berth in the capital city. When the excitement abated, she returned to sea duty for the repatriation of troops and other post-war priorities.

She returned to Belfast in 1947 for conversion to a commercial liner, to a standard which was even more modern than had been intended in 1939. When she left Southampton on her maiden trip on the following January 22, she was—as a result of the war casualties—the largest and fastest liner on the South American run. She was registered at 25,676 gross tons and, with her 21-knot service speed, she could travel from Southampton to Buenos Aires via Cherbourg, Lisbon, Las Palmas, Rio de Janeiro, Santos, and Montevideo in 16 days. Her berthing arrangements were balanced between 324 in high-standard First Class and 204 in a fairly comfortable Second Class.

There was no provision for a Third Class for immigrants which was instead handled by Royal Mail's 'Highland' class of liners. Aboard *Andes*, every cabin was on the outside and included were four de luxe suites and several cabins with a bed-sitting room arrangement. On deck, there was a well-attended outdoor pool, a theatre for late after-noon and evening performances, and (at a slightly later date) air-conditioning in the main restaurant and foyer.

Aside from the normal South American service to which she was teamed with the pre-war built *Alcantara*, the *Andes* was given over to cruising for at least several weeks each year. Her speciality was millionaire-style long-distance voyages that took her through the Mediterranean, to Scandinavia, and then further afield to South Africa, the Caribbean, California via Panama, Florida, and on one occasion on a transatlantic crossing to Bermuda and New York. Possibly one of her most unique trips was a short cruise from Southampton, along the southern coast, to represent Royal Mail at the Coronation Review at Spithead in June 1953. She was one of the largest of the 160 ships present in a fleet that stretched all the way to Cowes.

Andes closed out the South American service from Southampton in November 1959, in a company reshuffle that included basing the three brand-new sisters of the 'Amazon' class in London. The flagship—having reached two-thirds of her expected life—was sent to the De Schelde Shipyard in Vlissingen, Holland, for a major refit that would thereafter allow her to sail year-round in cruise service. The refit was rather unusual in that it was done in two stages with a 46-day run to the Caribbean and Florida in between. Her accommo-dation was thereafter merged into one class, all First, with 480 berths at most, in an extraordinary ratio to a 25,000-ton liner. When she left on her first official cruise, on June 10 1960, it was noted that she was Britain's first full-time cruise liner since 1939 (Cunard's cruise ship *Caronia* still made occasional port-to-port sailings as part of her near year-round holiday programme). The position of the *Andes* was secured quickly as one of the world's finest cruising vessels and one that had the status of a posh sea-going club.

When Royal Mail began evaluating plans for a replacement in the late 1960s, the outcome was greatly discoloured by the extreme rise in ship-building costs and even by the high costs of converting a second-hand, yet newer, ship to the standard of her predecessor. Operating costs were another consideration and probably dealt the final blow to any further thoughts on the subject. It was decided it would be far simpler for Royal Mail to abandon its passenger division completely. *Andes* was decommissioned in the spring of 1971 and arrived in Ghent on May 7, to be broken up by the firm of Van Heyghen Frères.

Gross tonnage: 25,689 (1939), 25,676 (1948), 25,895 (1960)
Length overall: 669 feet
Width: 83 feet
Draft: 29 feet
Machinery: Steam turbines geared to twin screw
Speed: 21 knots
Capacity: 403 First, 204 Second (as intended in 1939); 324 First, 204 Second (1948); 480 First (1960)
Built: Harland & Wolff Limited, Belfast, Northern Ireland, 1939
Demise: Scrapped in Ghent, Belgium, 1971

Above *The hull of the* Andes *was originally painted in black* (Courtesy of Alex Duncan).

Right *As a cruise ship, the* Andes *visited ports around the world. In this view, in Port Everglades, Florida, she is docked just aft of Cunard's* Carmania.

Below *In war-time colouring in Newport News, Virginia.*

Fifty Famous Liners

Andes

America

The *America* was a pre-war product that bowed into commercial service as a post-war symbol. The American passenger ship fleet of the 1930s consisted of numerous ships but was dominated on the North Atlantic by the sister ships *Washington* and *Manhattan*, and, for a short time, by the giant yet superfluous *Leviathan*. The latter liner suffered from economic instability, especially in those harsh Depression years of the early 1930s, and prompted the United States Lines to order a new third liner of somewhat smaller, more practical proportions. On October 21 1937, while the *Leviathan* was in her third year of 'lay-up' and still some months away from her final voyage to ship-breakers in Scotland, an order for this third ship was placed with the Newport News Shipbuilding and Dry Dock Company. William Francis Gibbs—one of the great twentieth-century marine designers—created plans for a very modern ship. The first keel plate was laid down on August 22 1938 and the sparkling new hull slid down the ways on August 31 1939 with Mrs Franklin Delano Roosevelt acting as the launch sponsor. On the following day, the peace-shattering invasion of Poland far overshadowed the excitement of the Newport News yard.

In the tense summer of 1940, the *America* ran her sea-trials and later was given a rousing reception in New York, her home port. One slight problem was immediately corrected. Her original funnels,

being rather squat in height, had to be raised to keep smoke off the aft decks. (It should be noted that only the second stack was a 'working' funnel. The forward one was simply a ventilator and served to balance the ship's profile.)

Regardless of the neutrality of the United States at the time, commercial operation to northern Europe, which was the *America*'s proposed trade, was impossible. The United States Lines, overcoming the possibility of lay up, placed the new liner in cruise service to the Caribbean and California via Panama. However, within a year, the *America* was called upon to serve her country. Her colourful profile was altered to dismal grey and, in an attempt at added security, she was renamed USS *West Point*. Plunged into the conflicts of war, the 8,175-passenger troop ship (increased from a capacity of 1,046 in peace time) began to be seen in ports around the world. Her entire war-time loggings were equivalent to nearly fifteen round-the-world voyages and her passenger record stood at 350,000, ranging from troops to war brides to medical patients. She visited Australia, India, South Africa, various parts of Europe, the American west coast, and passed through both the Panama and Suez Canals in her travels. Her military career had no major mishaps although there were several 'near misses'. While anchored off Singapore, enemy bombers came as close as 50 yards from the liner. Off Brazil, torpedoes closely crossed her bow and on other occasions, while in the Red Sea, off Australia, and at Port Suez, she was a near victim of enemy air attacks.

By the early part of 1946, the hard-worked and greatly reputed *West Point* was decommissioned from her war duties and thereafter proceeded to carry out her original purpose as an Atlantic passenger liner. Six million dollars' worth of reconditioning was necessary to bring the *America*, which had reverted to her famous name, to the highest standards. On November 14 1946, she departed on her first commerical crossing to Europe and in the years immediately following, despite original intentions, she worked single-handedly. Her status as flagship of the American merchant marine was greatly enhanced in this post-war era in that the United States then possessed the largest merchant fleet in the world (over 6,000 new ships were constructed during the war years alone).

America's superb operating performance was improved upon still further in the form of the 52,000-ton *United States*, delivered in the early summer of 1952. This record-breaker became the new American flagship and bore a slight resemblance to her predecessor. Thereafter, due to the considerable speed difference between the two ships, the *America* acted independently as a consort to the world's fastest liner. Both plied the Atlantic continuously, trading to the Channel ports of Southampton, Le Havre, and Cóbh and, on occasion, farther afield to Bremerhaven.

In the early 1960s, the *America* took up the part-time role, just as she had done very early in her career, of winter cruise ship to such ports as Bermuda, San Juan, and Nassau. The decline of the once great North-Atlantic liner trade was already well entrenched as the aircraft industry made successive inroads into the old-established services. With the *America*'s future uncertain as her load factors dwindled, a labour dispute among the crew over the use of toilet facilities erupted just hours before a noon-time departure in September 1963. No adequate settlement was reached and her passengers were forced ashore, only to spend several expensive days in New York hotels before catching the next European-bound liner. The problem for the 600 crew members persisted, despite embarrassing headlines and grave concern on the part of the United States Lines. With no hope for a quick resolution, the ship was towed across the Hudson to a Hoboken shipyard for what came to be a lengthy lay-up. For months, the *America* sat almost 'lifeless' as wild rumours spread that she would be retired permanently and possibly even sold off. Yet, in the following February, she returned to service to fulfil her schedule commitments.

When the official announcement came eight months later, in November 1964, that she had been sold for $1.5 million, American shipping prepared for a loss. She passed into the hands of Okeania S/A, a division of the ever-growing Chandris Group, and sailed to Piraeus for a major conversion. She was renamed *Australis*—'Australian maiden' according to her advertising—and outfitted with passenger berths for 2,258, all Tourist Class. Her new life was as queen of the Greek-Australian immigrant trade,

sailing outward from Southampton, through the Mediterranean (or via South Africa when the Suez was closed), and then on to Australia-New Zealand before returning via Mexico, Panama, the Caribbean, and Florida. Her gross tonnage jumped from 33,961 to 34,449, and she had the dubious distinction of carrying more passengers than any other liner then in service. While immigrants were her overall mainstay on the outward voyages, she also catered to world cruise passengers as well as Australians returning to Europe and Britain for holidays. She briefly flew the Panamanian flag before switching to Greek registry and had her hull colouring changed from black to white to grey.

Despite occasional cruises from both Southampton and Sydney, the *Australis* was competing again with the airlines during the 1970s on her immigrant and general liner voyages. Finally, in November 1978, she closed out the Chandris service to Australia and temporarily awaited her fate at anchor at Timaru, New Zealand. A strange and sad story followed. In January 1979, she was sold for $5 million to a new American travel firm listed as Venture Cruise Lines for short-distance sailings from New York. In an attempt to rekindle her past glory and appeal further to the US cruise market, she was renamed *America*, even despite her Greek flag. Once in New York, she was dry-docked briefly with hull and engines reported to be in good condition. However, the passenger interiors were in a desperate state of neglect. Her first voyage—a mini-cruise out to sea— was a scandalous affair with passengers reaching a state of near panic. The news media did not look kindly on the woes of the 38-year-old liner, even if she was the former flagship of the American fleet. The second sailing, again a short cruise, was equally disastrous with a variety of complaints ranging from 'unworkable' toilets to overbooking. In total humiliation, she was 'yanked' from service and laid up at her New York pier. Her short-lived owners were bankrupt and the ship was auctioned off by the United States District Court, which sold her for $1 million ($4 million less than the purchase price seven months before) to the Chandris Group, her original owners. She was ordered to Perama, near Piraeus in Greece, and laid up.

The Chandris firm revived her, under the name *Italis*, in the spring of 1979 and, with her forward funnel removed, she was assigned to two-week

Mediterranean cruise service, sailing mostly from Barcelona with Latin Americans that used special connecting air flights. It turned out to be a very brief assignment. By autumn, she had returned to Perama, for further lay-up and the inevitable scrapyard. Then, in 1980, there was something of a reprieve: conversion of the 40 year old liner to a hotel ship at a West African port. A year or so later, the former *America* was still laid-up at Perama, seemingly untouched. Evidently, there is still more of her story to come.

Gross tonnage: 33,532 (1949), 33,961 (1960)
Length overall: 723 feet
Width: 93 feet
Draft: 29 feet
Machinery: Steam turbines geared to twin screw
Speed: 22 knots
Capacity: 516 First, 371 Cabin, 159 Tourist; after 1960, revised to 516 First and 530 Tourist
Built: Newport News Shipbuilding & Dry Dock Company, Newport News, Virginia, 1940

Right *Being rebuilt after the war, a photo taken in Newport News, Virginia, on September 24 1946.*

Below *Idled by a strike in 1947, the* America *sits next to a US Lines 'Victory' ship at the company's Chelsea piers, Manhattan.*

America

Above *Being moved by Moran tugs as a 'dead ship' from Manhattan to Hoboken to await the end of another strike in 1963.*

Below *Toward the end of her sea-going career, the former* America *was renamed the* Italis *and had her forward 'dummy' stack removed* (Courtesy of A. Scrimali).

Queen Elizabeth

Cunard's brilliant scheme to have a two-ship trans-atlantic service with a sailing in each direction weekly produced the most famous pair of liners ever built. The *Queen Mary* came first and because of this and her record-breaking speed, she was always slightly the more famous, the more desirable among passengers and certainly given to one of the most glistening careers. The *Mary* came into service in the 1930s, the great age of the superliner, along with ships like the *Normandie*, the *Rex*, and the *Bremen*. She had a spectacular maiden voyage that received worldwide press and immediately established her reputation, prompting the statement that 'every schoolchild on both continents has heard of the *Queen Mary*.' The second half of this illustrious Cunard team, known almost everywhere simply as the 'Queens', did not experience this initial glamour. In fact, she arrived quietly and almost immediately went into war service.

The secrecy which surrounded the naming of the *Queen Mary* was not true of this second liner. *Queen Elizabeth* was publicly known to be the choice from the very beginning. The first keel plate was laid in position at the John Brown yards in Clydebank, Scotland, on December 4 1936. This new second liner would be quite different from the earlier one. She would look more modern, with two instead of three funnels, and the decks would be clear of the ventilators and other apparatus which seemed to crowd the upper portions on the *Mary*. The *Elizabeth* would have 12 boilers against the *Mary*'s 24. One of Cunard's technical engineers, disguised as a grocery clerk, made a trip in the *Normandie* and his findings proved to be far more influential in the design of the *Elizabeth* than even the *Queen Mary* was. The result represented quite a difference between Cunard's first and second express liners.

To begin with, the construction of the *Queen Elizabeth* was given priority. Shipyard crews worked round-the-clock, aided by huge floodlights attached to the cranes for the night shifts. On September 27 1938, the huge hull weighed 40,000 tons as Her Majesty Queen Elizabeth, accompanied by the Princesses Elizabeth (today the Queen) and Margaret, named the new liner and saw her launched. Actually, the ship began to move along the ways and into the River Clyde before the Queen had begun her speech. Fortunately, she was quick to release the bottle of champagne and to name the ship, even though the microphones thoughtlessly went dead. The liner moved to the fitting-out pier for the completion.

During the following year, as the political situation became increasingly serious, the finishing of the *Elizabeth* was no longer a shipyard priority. Many of the work gangs were reassigned to military ships. The liner's interiors were left unfinished, in vast shell-like conditions. Only essential plumbing and electrical work was completed, and even this only by special order from London. A proposal was made that she should be sold to the United States in her unfinished state. Some Members of Parliament saw her only as a major target for enemy bombers and thought her usefulness would only be ensured during peace-time. These were, of course, unjustified assumptions.

On February 6 1940 (her intended commercial maiden voyage was to begin on April 24), Winston Churchill ordered the unfinished ship away from Britain. New York was selected as a haven, where she could berth alongside the temporarily laid-up *Queen Mary*. This was, of course, a top-secret decision at the time. The dry dock in Southampton was alerted that the newest 'Queen' would be arriving for final outfitting. The scheme to mislead the Luftwaffe obviously worked. On the day that the *Queen Elizabeth* was due at Southampton, enemy bombers were discovered circling over the Channel. Fortunately, the liner, with a handful of shipyard workers still on board, was speeding across the North Atlantic for the safety of New York. The Nazis were furious.

The *Queen Elizabeth* finally reached New York on March 7. Work continued towards her completion but only as a 'passenger ship', since America was still technically neutral and preparation for military service was prohibited. The liner sat at her Manhattan pier for eight months before being ordered to the Pacific for final military outfitting. She was dry-docked in Singapore, in preference to Sydney where both of her masts would have had to be cut for bridge clearance. There was some talk that she was to be converted to an aircraft-carrier, a project to which Cunard strongly objected. Reconstruction of her interior could mean a capacity of 270 aircraft while a more modified plan showed accommodation for 6,000 troops and 48 aircraft. Fortunately, neither concept materialised.

The *Elizabeth* was at first assigned to Indian Ocean troop service, sailing between Sydney and Suez, Fremantle and Trincomalee. On her first such trip, in the spring of 1941, she departed from Sydney with 5,600 troops on board along with the *Queen Mary* with 6,000 and the *Mauretania* with 4,400.

In the early summer of 1942, the North African campaign was going badly and reinforcements for the Eighth Army were urgently needed. The 'Queens' were returned to the Atlantic, entering home waters by way of Cape Town and Rio de Janeiro before reaching New York. They were fitted out once again, this time to carry as many as 15,000 troops per weekly crossing. Their assignment was between New York and Gourock, Scotland. The ships were given tiered 'standee' bunks that were stretcher-like contraptions made of canvas slung between poles. These required a minimum amount of space and were arranged as many as six high. Consequently, a former two-berth stateroom could hold ten times that number. These standees were placed in the former lounges as well and only two dining rooms and two saloons were retained as open spaces. Some 8,000 service personnel could sleep at any given time while a second 'sleep shift' could hold a further 8,000.

Both 'Queens' were meticulously guarded. The crew members were hand selected. Seven-hundred-and-fifty guards were used at the New York pier yet even so beer-bottle caps were found stuck in the nozzles of the fire hoses aboard the *Elizabeth* and later holes discovered in several lifeboats which when lowered promptly sank. Two bombs were found on board, buried in a pile of blankets, in April 1943. They were immediately thrown overboard.

In all, both 'Queens' gave impeccable war-time service and miraculously survived. The *Elizabeth*, selected to be the symbol of peace-time, returned to Southampton on June 16 1946, to undergo restoration. Her military equipment was removed and large consignments of furniture and other materials were unloaded from warehouses throughout Britain. In the end, all the peace-time items were gathered together in one huge warehouse for final sorting and assignment. Work went on round-the-clock. Some 21,000 separate pieces of furniture were placed aboard, including 4,500 couches, chairs, and tables. These were 6,000 pairs of curtains and bedspreads, and a further 2,000 carpets. The *Queen Elizabeth*—now over six years old—finally left Southampton on her commercial maiden voyage on October 16 1946. She was joined by the *Mary* in the following summer and the two-ship weekly Atlantic service went into operation.

The 'Queens' were the most spectacularly profitable pair of liners ever built and headed the great Cunard fleet. The Line was said to carry one-third of all Atlantic sea-going passengers during the 1950s and at one point, during 1958, had twelve passenger ships in service to the United States and Canada.

Both 'Queens' began to show deficits in the early 1960s, just as jet airliners were firmly succeeding in their takeover on the North-Atlantic run. Cunard was thinking, however, in terms of a large liner to replace the *Mary* and sent the *Elizabeth* into dry dock in the winter of 1965–6 for a major overhaul that would ensure her survival until 1975. She would be the running-mate, at least for a time, to the new 'Queen'. The *Elizabeth* was fitted with a large stern lido deck and swimming pool, given complete air-conditioning and considerably more private plumbing to her passenger cabins. However, despite more time spent on supposedly more lucrative cruising, she continued to show staggering losses. When it was decided to retire the *Mary* in September

Fifty Famous Liners

1967, the decision included her running-mate. The *Elizabeth* came off the Atlantic trade in October 1968.

Following somewhat in the *Mary*'s footsteps, the *Queen Elizabeth* was sent to America for intended use as a floating hotel, convention centre, and museum. She was berthed in Port Everglades, Florida, and her American buyers (Cunard still had an 85 per cent interest in her) proposed that she could be the Atlantic end of the illustrious 'matching pair'—the *Mary* in California, the *Elizabeth* in Florida. What a tourist bonanza—or so they thought! Two years came to pass. There were deep financial problems and the *Elizabeth* continued to deteriorate—rusted, sun-scorched, mostly neglected. Finally, she was placed on auction and, in September 1970, sold to Taiwanese shipping tycoon C Y Tung. His plan was to rebuild her as a floating university that toured the world. She was renamed *Seawise University* (Seawise being a variation of the owner's initials, C Y Tung) and registered under the Bahamian flag. The voyage out to Hong Kong via the Caribbean and South Africa was tedious and marred by a series of mechanical breakdowns, one of which left the liner anchored off Aruba for two months awaiting repairs.

A year later, on January 9 1972, the former 'Queen' had undergone $6 million worth of refitting and was lying in Hong Kong harbour, shortly to sail to Japan for dry-docking and then to begin her maiden voyage. Fire suspiciously broke out and spread rapidly throughout the ship. Fireboats and other craft poured vast amounts of water onto her but with the same careless miscalculation that had ruined the *Normandie* exactly 30 years earlier. The next morning, the *Seawise University* turned on its side and capsized. She was a total loss.

Talks of salvage and possible rebuilding were based more on optimism than reality. In the end, her only hope was scrapping on the spot. Today, in lower New York, in front of the C Y Tung building, there stands a sculpture in tribute to the *Queen Elizabeth*. Her record was one of the greatest of all transatlantic liners.

Gross tonnage: 83,673 (1940), 82,998 (1965)
Length overall: 1,031 feet
Width: 118 feet
Draft: 38 feet
Machinery: Steam turbines geared to quadruple screw
Speed: 28.5 knots
Capacity: 823 First, 662 Cabin, 798 Tourist
Built: John Brown & Company Limited, Clydebank, Scotland, 1940
Demise: Burned and capsized in Hong Kong, January 9-10 1972; scrapped on the spot 1974

The 'Queen' just one month before her launching, August 1938.

Fifty Famous Liners

Above *The* Elizabeth *inbound in New York, September 1962.*
Left *Following a 'secret' maiden voyage across the Atlantic, she is safely eased into Pier 90, Manhattan. The* Queen Mary *and the* Normandie *are docked in the background.*
Below *Aground overnight at the entrance to Southampton harbour with 2,246 passengers and 1,200 crew aboard.*

Willem Ruys

The *Willem Ruys* had one of the most fascinating silhouettes of all passenger liners. For many years Holland's second largest liner, she represented an unconventional yet handsome vessel. With a battle-ship-grey hull and white superstructure, her masts were coated in pink and her twin pear-shaped funnels in solid black. Her lifeboats were stowed inboard, a feature quite novel when she was introduced in 1947 and later best exemplified in P & O's *Canberra* and *Oriana*.

The *Willem Ruys* was originally contracted in 1939, by Rotterdam Lloyd in response to the rival Nederland Line's *Oranje*. While in the earliest stages of construction at the yards of Royal De Schelde in Flushing, Holland was invaded and building halted. When the enemy gave orders to resume work, it was carried on at a deliberately slow pace and partially sabotaged on several occasions by the Dutch Underground. When the Nazi forces retreated, it was sheer luck that the partially complete vessel was not destroyed.

By 1946, the ships of the Rotterdam Lloyd were lying in ports around the world in various degrees of decay. Therefore, the completion of the new flagship was listed as a priority. When construction resumed, it was decided that she would be named *Willem Ruys*, in tribute to the company director who had been murdered as an enemy hostage. Ruys directors had been with the firm since its inception in 1839 when running sailing ships to Batavia.

In November 1947, the *Willem Ruys* was sent into the North Sea to run her sea-trials. Emerging with a top speed of 24.62 knots, she deserved the honour of being Holland's first post-war luxury liner. On November 21, at the time of the ship's transfer to her owners, Her Majesty Queen Wilhelmina granted the company a 'royal prefix' for its valuable service rendered during the war. Thus, the *Willem Ruys* was the new flagship of the Royal Rotterdam Lloyd.

Accommodation was divided into four classes— First, Second, Third, and Fourth—and provided a total capacity of 840 berths. Making Rotterdam as her home port, she sailed out via Southampton, the Mediterranean, Suez, and Aden on voyages to Indonesia. Her chief rival, the 20,100-ton *Oranje*,

sailed from Amsterdam on a very similar service. It is interesting to note that during 1953, while in the Red Sea, the *Oranje* collided with the *Willem Ruys*, resulting in damages that forced both ships into port for repairs.

Following the political difficulties in Indonesia during the 1950s, the traffic requirements that had once supported the *Willem Ruys* dwindled to a mere fraction of the original level. By 1958, it was decided that the Royal Rotterdam Lloyd would enter into a cooperative agreement with the rival Nederland Line and create a round-the-world passenger service. Together with the *Willem Ruys*, the *Oranje* and the 19,700-ton *Johan Van Oldenbarnevelt* would undergo refitting in preparation. Just prior to arriving at the shipyard, the *William Ruys* made two transatlantic voyages to Montreal as part of a charter to the Europe-Canada Line.

From September 20 until February 25 1959, 2,000 technicians and workmen balanced day and night shifts to complete the extensive overhaul. Regarding the modernisation, her owners wisely considered that the *Willem Ruys* must compete viably with liners already in the worldwide trade. Original class distinctions were dropped in favour of a new First and Tourist Class (the addition of 100 new cabins increased the overall capacity to 1,167). Cargo areas were sharply decreased to provide space

for the new cabin accommodation. The initial Javanese crewmen were replaced by Europeans and therefore more modern crew quarters were constructed. Additionally, the liner was made fully air-conditioned, a system which required 15,000 kilometers of piping. Denny Brown stabilisers, a new evaporator plant, and new auxiliary engines were fitted. Public rooms were refurbished while several additional rooms were created. Some of her decks were increased in size and the funnels were raised ten feet in height to keep smoke and soot off the open aft areas.

The *Willem Ruys* was returned to her owners on February 27 as a more modern and larger ship (the gross tonnage having jumped from 21,100 to 23,100). Shortly thereafter, she left on her first world sailing. Her itinerary read: Rotterdam, Southampton, Port Said, Suez, Colombo, Singapore, Melbourne, Sydney, Wellington, Callao, Balboa, Cristobal, Port Everglades, Bermuda, Southampton, and back to Rotterdam. The schedule required 63/64 days for a complete sailing and was so arranged to have the ship in Rotterdam for the Christmas holidays.

However, the new service was short-lived. The frequency of sailings by the three liners was not sufficient to build a loyal following among the sea-minded travelling public. Passenger loads were therefore often light and the trio became economic burdens to their owners. By 1963, Nederland Line had retired the *Johan Van Oldenbarnevelt.* Several months later, a similar fate was determined for the *Oranje* and *Willem Ruys*, and both ships were placed on the sales lists. Thanks to their extremely good condition, they were sold almost immediately to Flotta Lauro of Naples and, by the end of 1964, they were in their new owner's hands and were sent to Italian shipyards for renovations.

The Lauro interests had been planning two 27,000-ton liners at the time of purchasing the two Dutch liners. In view of the potential in both the *Oranje* and the *Willem Ruys*, the building plans were abandoned and the two second-hand ships renovated to suit Lauro's vast interests in the Australia–New Zealand trade. Lavish new designs were created. However, one serious and very ironic situation caused something of a set-back. In August 1965, while lying at separate Italian yards, both liners were swept by fire, within days of each other. Repairs

took place and the ships were finally introduced in the spring of 1966.

Honouring the Lauro Line founder, owner, and one-time Mayor of Naples, the *Willem Ruys* was christened the *Achille Lauro.* At first sight, she did not seem to be the same ship. She had new sleek funnels with large smoke-deflecting wings. Her single mast was placed above the bridge and the aft decks smoothed to create a substantial lido area. Her interiors were redecorated in colourful Mediterranean themes and the cabin accommodation was enlarged, with berths for 1,728 passengers.

Initially, the *Achille Lauro* and the former *Oranje* (which had been renamed *Angelina Lauro*) were assigned to sailings out of Bremerhaven, Rotterdam, Southampton, Genoa, Naples, and Messina to Port Said, Aden, Fremantle, Melbourne, Sydney, and Wellington, with return via the same ports. Then, following the 1967 closure of the Suez Canal, they began sailing via Cape Town, with occasional homeward trips via the Strait of Magellan, Buenos Aires, and Rio de Janeiro. Furthermore, cruises were offered from Australian ports to the South Pacific and from north European cities to Scandinavia.

Air competition killed off most of the last remains of the Australian passenger-ship trade by 1972. Both Lauro liners were taken in hand by Italian shipyards and upgraded for full-time cruise service. In May of that year, while at a Genoa repair dock, the *Achille Lauro* was again seriously damaged by a fire but again it was economically viable to repair her. She was back in service by December. One further incident occurred in April 1975 when she rammed and sank a small Lebanese freighter off Turkey.

Her cruise operations are mostly within the Mediterranean, on two-week trips from Genoa, but each winter she sails on longer, more de luxe voyages that have taken her to South America, Africa, the Middle East, and completely around the world.

Gross tonnage: 21,119 (1947), 23,114 (1959)
Length overall: 631 feet
Width: 82 feet
Draft: 29 feet
Machinery: Sulzer diesels geared to twin screw
Speed: 22 knots
Capacity: 840 First, Second, Third and Fourth (1947); 1,167 First and Tourist (1959)
Built: Royal De Schelde Shipyard, Flushing, Holland, 1947

Postcard photos of the Willem Ruys. *Note the lifeboats slung from a lower-than-usual deck. Although built after the* Oranje, *she had the traditional mainmast.*

Above *The unusual stern is shown as she steams into New York harbour for the first time. Note that a lifeboat has been added to the upperdeck aft, not in place on previous postcard photos.*

Below *As the* Achille Lauro, *the original* Willem Ruys *was greatly changed* (Courtesy of Alex Duncan).

United States

The *United States* was the lifetime creation of a remarkable man named William Francis Gibbs. Passionately fond of ships from his earliest days, he studied law, passed his bar examinations, and practised for two years, spending all his free time teaching himself the skills of naval architecture and marine engineering. Abandoning law, he determined to build the world's first 1,000-foot, 30-knot liner. With extraordinary motivation he managed to prove himself first to one and then another important person in the marine field. In 1916, as his first working assignment, he won the right to design his dream ship, being commissioned to this task by the world's largest passenger liner company of that day, the International Mercantile Marine. This ship eventually became the *United States.*

Between 1916 and the late 1940s Gibbs's fame grew. He rebuilt the *Leviathan*; he designed many famous liners from the *Malolo* to the *America*; he led the battle for high-pressure boilers in naval vessels; and all the while he did engineering studies for 'the big ship'. But there were obstacles. The era of the fast liner was nearly over; American maritime labour unions were at the peak of their power; the United States Congress had little interest in merchant ships, and Gibbs knew that 70 per cent of the cost of a superliner would have to be government-authorised.

In addition to a determination to overcome all odds, Gibbs was a perfectionist, and he had a passion for safety at sea. He had spent a lifetime studying the *Titanic*'s sinking and the burning of the *Morro Castle*. He would build the strongest, most fire-proof, and fastest liner ever constructed.

The maximum construction subsidy he could expect was about half the cost, and so, with Navy cooperation, Gibbs devised a way of getting yet another large chunk of financial help. He explained that the liner would need 'national defence' features: two engine rooms for insurance against torpedo attacks, extra speed for her service as a troop ship, etc. The cost of these features was added to the sum requested from Washington. His success in this area created another problem. So completely did the government and the public accept the concept that the *United States* would be a thinly disguised troop ship that many were brainwashed into thinking she really was not intended to be a luxury liner at all. Changing this attitude was one of the big public relations difficulties her owners were to have but they eventually succeeded.

On her trials in 1952 the *United States* lived up to all the expectations of her perfectionist designer. Although he wrapped a thick blanket of secrecy about her, she proved that she could easily break the Atlantic record. Her top speed was recorded as 38.32 knots, developing 241,785 shaft horsepower. This, of course, was kept a secret for many years. On her maiden voyage she succeeded in establishing new Atlantic speed records in both directions.

The question of the tonnage of the *United States* has puzzled many. She came out as the third largest liner in the world with a gross of 53,329 tons. It was the story of the *Leviathan* all over again. Gibbs was determined to make her have as great a gross tonnage as possible for advertising and publicity value. He used the British measurement and also included in his computing every possible extra he could justify as permanently enclosed earning area. Years later it was revealed that under a strict interpretation of the American rules, with no padding, she measured only 38,216 gross tons. The difference in ways of measuring gross makes a fair comparison of ships by their tonnage alone almost

Co-author Braynard is among the group standing above the bridge in this photo from the sea-trials.

impossible. The vessel was longer even than the QE2, being surpassed by only four other liners in all time.

The great success of the *United States* was not only in her reputation for safety or because of her speed, but in her actual record as a passenger carrier. Although she was of slightly less capacity than the two British 'Queen' liners, she regularly carried more passengers than they did, if their lists were averaged together. In her first full year of service she carried 69,231 passengers, while the *Mary* carried 63,443 and the *Elizabeth* carried 70,775.

As time passed her competitive position improved and she regularly carried more passengers than any other ship in the world. But two factors brought about her downfall. The supersonic aeroplane was put into service on the Atlantic and from that moment point-to-point travel by liner was doomed. More and more people chose the quick, if less comfortable way to travel to and from Europe, and went by air. Labour problems continued to get worse. Tug strikes, dock strikes, and strikes by seamen cut into the remarkable record the *United States* was making for herself. William Francis Gibbs

continued to have his 'love affair' with 'the big ship' as he always called her. He would telephone her Master and her Chief Engineer every day they were at sea. And he visited her at just about every sailing and arrival. His passing in 1967 prevented his seeing her withdrawn from service late in 1969 when continuous labour problems forced US Lines to lay her up.

At the time of writing there is a possibility that 'the big ship' will once again sail. She has been bought by a company which wishes to put her into cruise service. Fortunately, she was well taken care of during her 12 years of lay-up. When dry-docked in 1980 her hull was said to be just about as good as new.

Gross tonnage: 53,329
Length overall: 990 feet
Width: 101.6 feet
Draft: 31 feet
Machinery: Steam turbines geared to quadruple screw
Speed: 35 knots (maximum 38.23)
Capacity: 913 First, 558 Cabin, 537 Tourist
Built: Newport News Shipbuilding & Dry Dock Company, Newport News, Virginia, USA, 1952

Left *This view, kept secret for nearly two decades, shows the starboard propellers of the* United States— *the outer one having four blades, the inner one five.*

Below left *Docking the great liners, particularly on icy winter mornings, demanded the greatest skill* (Courtesy of Moran Towing).

Right *View of the* United States *at Southampton's Western Docks with the* Athlone Castle *and the* Queen Mary *further along* (Courtesy of the British Transport Commission).

Below *Inbound in Southampton—with the troop ship* Dilwara *and the liner* Queen Elizabeth *in the background* (Courtesy of British Transport Commission).

Santa Maria

Certain liners are especially well known because of one thing that happened during their lives. The *Egypt* is remembered because gold was salvaged from her sunken hull, the *Republic* because of the first use of wireless, the *Principessa Julanda* because she sank at the moment of her launching, and the *Waratah* because she was lost without trace. None of these has any more claim to fame, however, than the Portuguese liner the *Santa Maria*. She was hijacked!

At least four books have been written about the 1961 episode that gave her the attention of the world for 12 days. Two were paperbacks; the others were serious historical works. One took one side and defended the hijackers, showing them as political heroes; the other was written with sympathy for the government of Antonio de Salazar.

The *Santa Maria*, owned by the Companhia Colonial de Navegaçao, of Lisbon, was well ahead of her time in design. Great use was made of aluminium and as a result her superstructure was larger and more commodious than that of other vessels of her day. Her 'built-up' appearance suggested much later cruise-liner design. Most interesting interiors distinguished this handsome vessel. Very fine murals, striking colour combinations and wall hangings, wood carvings of Portuguese saints, and superb panelling with intricate inlaid woods from many parts of Africa, gave her and her sister, the *Vera Cruz*, most distinctive atmospheres. Like all Portuguese liners, she was very sedate, very conservative, very elegant! She was popular on the run to South America. Then she was shifted to steam over a giant triangle, linking Portugal with Madeira, the Canaries, La Guaira, Curaçao, and Port Everglades. Her stop in Florida introduced her to many Americans who sailed on her eastwards back to Lisbon.

She was serving this triangular run in 1961 when she went through 'one of the most remarkable dramas in the history of steam navigation', in the words of British nautical scholar, Noel R P Bonsor. Those interested in the full story should read the two serious books on the matter: Warren Rogers Jr, American journalist, gave the pro-rebel side of the affair in his excellent book *The Floating Revolution* (McGraw-Hill, NY, 1962), and freelance writer, Beth Day, told the story from the owners' standpoint in her *Passage Perilous* (Putnam, NY, 1962).

The drama began with her departure from Lisbon on January 9. She called at Vigo, Spain, Madeira, Tenerife, La Guaira, and Curaçao. On board were 612 perfectly ordinary seeming passengers, but 24 of them were far from ordinary. They were revolutionaries under the leadership of Henrique Carlos Malta Galvao. Rogers describes this gentleman as 'the almost legendary soldier, bureaucrat, big-game hunter, playwright, novelist, rebel, fugitive and implacable foe' of Salazar. Authoress Beth Day introduced Galvao by noting that most Portuguese were 'inclined to laugh indulgently at his periodic exploits' and she added that 'he was always in the news, involved in some romantic scandal or grandiose scheme.'

On Sunday, January 22, while sailing through the calm Caribbean, the rebels showed themselves. A fight ensued and the ship's Third Mate, Nascimento Costa, was fatally shot. In minutes, the ship was under the rigid control of the Galvao party. For the next 11 days she was front-page news. Her whereabouts were unknown for four days, despite the frantic efforts of the US Navy and Air Force to find her. Eventually she was spotted by a resourceful television news photographer named Herbert Schwartz, who had chartered a plane on his own and gone out looking. Once she was found the saga petered out into a series of radio messages between the US Navy, Brazilian authorities, and Galvao.

When it became apparent that the ship was running out of fuel and that an all-out battle with her 365 crew members and nearly 600 legitimate passengers could only result in bloodshed and final defeat for the small band of rebels, Galvao agreed to put into Recife, Brazil. The Santa Maria was given back to her master, Captain Mario Simoes Maia. Galvao, boasting unconvincing, home-made admiral's epaulets, faded into obscurity. The liner steamed back home where, on February 16, she was welcomed by 150,000 cheering Portuguese. The affair may possibly have played a small part in arousing feeling for the eventual revolution in Portugal, although Salazar himself remained in power until he had a stroke in 1968. The *Santa Maria* served with credit until retired in 1973.

Gross tonnage: 20,906
Length overall: 608.9 feet
Width: 75.8 feet
Draft: 27.8 feet
Machinery: Steam, double reduction-geared turbines, twin screw
Speed: 20 knots
Capacity: 156 First, 228 Cabin, 696 Tourist
Built: John Cockerill, Hoboken, Holland, 1953
Demise: Scrapped in Taiwan, 1973

A side view of the Santa Maria, *showing her modern-style outline—high superstructure far forward, mast above the bridge, no mainmast.*

Left *The First-Class dining room* (Courtesy of Companhia Colonial).

Right *The* Santa Maria *had her name spelled out in electric letters on the top deck between the mast and funnel* (Courtesy of Companhia Colonial).

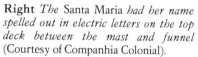

Below right *With flags flying* (Courtesy of Bill Rau).

Left *A de luxe cabin in First Class* (Courtesy of Companhia Colonial).

Santa Maria

Andrea Doria

It was 4 am when I was awakened by the telephone on Thursday, July 26 1956. A television station was on the wire asking me to come into New York and talk about collisions on the *Will Rogers Jr Show*. There had been a collision off Nantucket, I was told. Without asking what ships were involved I said 'yes' and started dressing. It took me only 45 minutes to drive into the Grand Central Station studio, half the time it usually took in traffic. I even found a parking place. Rushing into the studio I came to a news ticker and read the names S-T-O-C-K-H-O-L-M and A-N-D-R-E-A D-O-R-I-A!

I was introduced to a tallish chap with glasses and a smiling face, Walter Lord, author of *A Night To Remember*. We were guests on the show for the next two early-morning hours. We drew diagrams of other collisions, discussed the size and construction of the two ships involved, and read news-ticker reports as they came in describing the rescue operations. Neither of us dreamed that either ship would sink, certainly not the great new Italian liner. Both of us had been aboard her and knew her well. When the programme was over we walked across the street for breakfast at the Yale Club, where Walter Lord was a member. Then I hurried downtown to my 11 Broadway office. Shortly after 10 am my *Herald Tribune* newspaper friend, Walter Hamshar, called to shock me with the words: 'She's gone!'

I went over to the Italian Line office on State Street to try to help. In the afternoon while still there I noticed some people staring out of the windows. They were looking (with 'daggers in their eyes') at the *Stockholm*, limping in, her bow smashed. The arrival that evening of the *Ile de France*, which I also saw, was entirely different. Every ship in the harbour saluted her as she brought in the bulk of those rescued.

As a ship, the *Andrea Doria* was a striking and beautiful vessel. Italian naval architects have had a distinctive, classical style with their great liners, and this was very evident with the *Andrea Doria*. Her exterior lines were simple, yet grand. Her interiors were on the ornate side, although the public loved them in her three years of life. The bridal suite was definitely overdone, leaving a feeling of too-much-of-a-good-thing. Signs of the zodiac and mythical astrological creatures were everywhere on walls, floors, rugs, ceilings, even on the inside of every object in the bathroom, including the bidet. They were all done in blue and white, and no other colours of any kind were to be seen in the suite, except for a red-rose design above the huge headboard uniting the large, side-by-side twin beds.

Much has been written about the collision. The official American inquiry was abruptly interrupted when the two steamship lines settled out of court. Much controversy remains. Among the very few facts that stood out was the cardinal one that both sides were to blame. Both ships were speeding in dense fog, both were poorly handled. Both sides eventually accepted partial guilt. As the Italian Line lost much more in the sinking of their ship, the settlement has been accepted as an admission of a larger share of guilt by them. In the long run the public was the chief loser for 51 lives were lost. The two shipping lines were protected by legal jargon and limited liability clauses and the relatives of those who died were forced to accept pennies.

Like the *Titanic*, the *Andrea Doria* has become tremendously famous, far more so than she might have been had she survived to a ripe old age and been retired like her sister, the *Cristoforo Colombo*. She remains for posterity one of history's best-known liners. A continuous series of efforts to salvage her supposed treasures followed her loss. A number of lives were lost in these attempts and finally the interest in this sort of effort seemed to peter out. Nevertheless, one of the most common questions that I am asked is: 'Do you think that they will ever raise the *Andrea Doria?*' And the controversy over the accident and who was to blame will never end. Why was the *Stockholm* in the wrong lane? Why was her Master never called to the bridge? Why did the *Doria* fail to make the fullest use of radar? Why did she violate the rule of the road and turn to port so as to pass the *Stockholm* starboard-to-starboard? The farther the disaster recedes into history the more bizarre the stories are that surface; for example, the August *New York Times* published on its front page late in 1980 an utterly unsubstantiated charge by a very pro-*Stockholm* Swedish writer that Italian officials had bribed the classification societies so the *Andrea Doria* could win permission to operate. Very sad!

Gross tonnage: 29,082
Length overall: 700 feet
Width: 90.2 feet
Draft: 30 feet
Machinery: Steam turbine, twin screw
Speed: 23 knots
Capacity: 218 First, 320 Cabin, 703 Tourist
Built: Società Anonima Ansaldo, Genoa, Italy, 1952
Demise: Sunk in collision on July 26 1956

Just hours before launching in Genoa, June 16 1952.

Above *A rare occasion when the* Andrea Doria *and her sister ship, the* Cristoforo Colombo, *were docked together in Genoa, stern in as was the universal custom there for liners.*

Below *The liner listing, near the end. The American transport* Pvt William H Thomas *awaits further survivors.*

Canberra

In May 1960, the legendary Peninsular & Oriental Steam Navigation Company Limited (P & O) merged with the Orient Steam Navigation Company and the combination created the largest passenger-ship fleet on earth: 16 liners—*Orsova, Oronsay, Orcades, Orion, Orontes, Iberia, Arcadia, Himalaya, Chusan, Canton, Stratheden, Strathmore, Strathnaver, Strathaird, Corfu,* and *Carthage.* Its worldwide service, although primarily linked to Australia and the East, was still showing most encouraging profits. It was unlike the Atlantic where the inroads of the airline industry were beginning seriously to worry companies like Cunard, which was still maintaining an 11-liner fleet. The freshly created P & O-Orient Lines could only look forward to promising times.

The merger was considered particularly timely since both firms were constructing their largest passenger ships yet, Orient having the 41,000-ton *Oriana* on the ways in Barrow-in-Furness and P & O the even larger *Canberra* in Belfast. These ships were the biggest built in Britain since the *Queen Elizabeth* in 1940, and were justifiably hailed as the nation's latest sea queens. The tone of the new liners was nothing if not revolutionary. Orient Line chose a rather eccentric appearance for their *Oriana*, with one funnel higher than the other and both of a different shape, a series of upper-deck arrangements that often resembled an apartment block, and only a shortish radar mast forward. However, her innards were praised for their superb sense of coordination and flow. Deck spaces abounded and her machinery made her the fastest ever to Australia. She was, in fact, the first new liner under British flag that could stand in for one of the Atlantic 'Queens'.

Meanwhile, P & O's *Canberra*—some 3,000 tons larger and statistically the biggest liner ever built for a service other than the North Atlantic—was beautifully streamlined despite the disappearance of the conventional funnel replaced by raked, twin uptakes aft. Her lifeboats were stowed inboard at a level a full three decks lower than normally expected. She offered unequalled open-air deck spaces and was powered by the more unique steam turbo-electric machinery (similar to the *Normandie* and just a handful of others), as against the more traditional steam turbine or diesel drive used in other passenger ships.

The *Oriana* and *Canberra* not only represented the culmination of P & O-Orient's long experience in passenger-ship design but hinted at the future. Their operations would not be limited to Australia and the East but would have more of a worldwide scope, both in the form of regular liner voyages and single-class cruising. Particular attention was paid to the transpacific route which, according to company forecasts at the time, would continue to boom with travellers especially from North America. P & O-Orient considered the entire Pacific as the last frontier of ocean-liner travel.

The *Canberra* was launched amidst great attention on March 16 1960, at the Harland & Wolff yards. Dame Pattie Menzies, wife of the then Prime Minister of Australia, was the sponsor and performed the naming ceremony, attaching a sprig of white heather (which she had carried 6,000 miles from home) to the ribbons fastened to the bottle of Australian christening wine. Because of her size and outstanding design, the ship was a matter of

particular pride to all present, from the P & O-Orient Board to the shipyard work crews. She was very much the new flagship.

Her immediate nickname was 'the ship that shapes the future'. She had bow propellers for easier manoeuvring and with the use of aluminium her overall tonnage was reduced by 1,500 tons yet had the facility for 200 additional passenger cabins. Special baggage conveyors were installed as well as twin sets of stabilisers, and there was far more private plumbing in her accommodation than any previous P & O liner. There were three outdoor pools (one for First Class and two for Tourist), a full theatre and a Tourist-Class restaurant large enough to take 704 passengers at a single sitting.

Glistening and fresh, she left Belfast for her trials on April 29 1961 and recorded a run of 29.27 knots, nearly two full knots above her intended operating speed. She was briefly dry-docked in Southampton prior to the official handing over on May 19. She left Southampton on her maiden voyage on June 2, for a 90-day cruise around the world, sailing outward to Australia via Suez and then homeward via North America and Panama. She departed with a full capacity of 2,238 passengers (the highest at the time for a major liner) of which 820 were immigrants, 200 bound for local Mediterranean ports and the remainder for other ports along the run or for the complete voyage. All seemed well.

A major mechanical breakdown some 160 miles off Malta on January 5 1963 seemed to tarnish the glitter. Her voyage had to be cancelled and she was forced back to Southampton and then to dry dock in Belfast. Although repairs were made, the *Canberra* remained a 'tender' ship with a certain degree of operating difficulties, one of which was her buoyancy which necessitated filling parts of her hull with cement. Consequently, the *Oriana*—as her chief running-mate—was established as the better running ship of the two. However, the *Canberra* developed great popularity. She had a yearly quota of Australian sailings, which were often extended to make full round-the-world voyages, as well as cruises, which included several trips to New York.

By 1972, the problems that had hit the North

Atlantic, namely competition from the air, had reached the Australian and worldwide passenger trades. Specifically, the introduction of inexpensive airline charter fares was particularly injurious to the future of many steamship companies. P & O had to re-evaluate its position and began by sending the eighteen-year-old *Iberia* to the scrapyards of Taiwan. Others of the immediate post-war fleet would have to be retired as well and, even more frightening, the roles of the still relatively new *Canberra* and *Oriana* would be examined. The results included a new experimental service for the *Canberra*.

She was sent to New York in January 1973 to begin year-round cruising, mostly on one and two-week jaunts to the Caribbean. With little effort, her class divisions were dropped and facilities joined to make a single 'holiday class' for 1,737 passengers. Marketing was co-ordinated with Cunard, which had far more experience in the New York trade. Sadly, the results were quite unsatisfactory. The *Canberra* carried far too few passengers in her new service, to the point where she was laid up during February and

Right *The staggering lines of the* Canberra *as she is assisted into her Manhattan pier* (Courtesy of Moran Towing).

Fifty Famous Liners

March at an empty berth in Wilmington, North Carolina. When she resumed cruising, there were more problems. She was aground for three days at Grenada, in the West Indies, from July 12. A month or so later, on August 14, she grounded once again at the entrance to St Thomas harbour. By September, she had returned to Southampton, awaiting reassignment. Rumours in high-ranking P & O circles suggested that she was far too large for cruising and costly during the fuel crisis and then repeated reference was made to her 'tender' operating condition. Some thought was even given to converting the 29,000-ton *Orsova* for year-round cruising and condemning the *Canberra* to the scrap heap. Then, following a rather extensive re-examination, the *Canberra* was spared. (The *Orsova* was, by the way, scrapped in Taiwan at the end of 1974.)

The *Canberra* and the *Oriana* were permanently re-styled as one-class cruise ships, based in Southampton mostly for two and three-week runs to the Mediterranean, the Canaries, West Africa, Scandinavia, and the Caribbean. Consequently, the *Canberra* has appeared in an even greater variety of world ports, from Spitzbergen to Rio, the Azores to Haifa. Each winter, in January, she makes something of a nostalgic world cruise that is now (in 1981) filled more with return-trip holiday passengers than port-to-port voyagers. In the twenty years since her completion, she and the *Oriana* survive as the last of the P & O-Orient liners of that earlier style. Today, she is engaged in a trade that has undergone enormous change.

Gross tonnage: 45,733 (1961), 44,807 (1968)
Length overall: 818 feet
Width: 102 feet
Draft: 32 feet
Machinery: Steam turbo-electric engines geared to twin screw
Speed: 27.5 knots
Capacity: 556 First and 1,716 Tourist passengers adjustable to 596 First and 1,616 Tourist; 1,737 one-class for cruising after 1972
Built: Harland & Wolff Limited, Belfast, Northern Ireland, 1961

Canberra

Right *One of today's great ladies of the sea—the* Canberra *(Courtesy of Moran Towing).*

Left *As with most P&O–Orient liners, the outdoor spaces are particularly plentiful.*

Right *The Cricketer's Tavern is one of 16 lounges aboard the* Canberra.

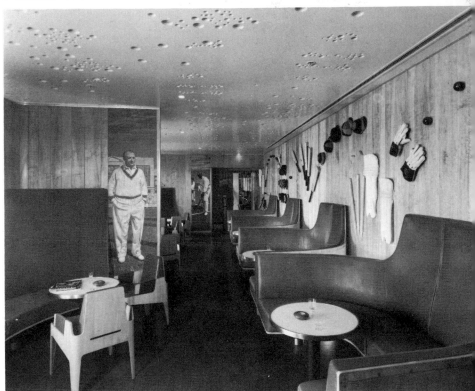

France

The *France* was the last superliner designed for the North Atlantic that would spend most of her year on that trade; off-season, winter cruising was on the whole not included in the planning. Furthermore, and in all due respect to Cunard's *Queen Elizabeth 2*, the *France* was the final member of that regal, class-divided type of transatlantic flagship in which select travellers were accommodated in vast, luxury suites and cabins along the upper decks while a larger and less pretentious Tourist Class catered to what one French Line official called 'the affluent working class'. Despite the waning of the Atlantic-liner trade, the *France* remained a symbol of luxury—opulent, well-fed, impeccably reputed.

She took 4 years, 3 months and 28 days to create. The French government, which was deeply concerned with the tragedy of Algeria, saw the liner as something of an impressive morale-builder. It extended a $14 million loan to the French Line, the nation's biggest steamship company and one more formally known as the Compagnie Générale Transatlantique. The firm would furnish the remaining $66 million. The initial construction studies insisted that one 66,000-ton liner would be far superior to two, more conventional 30,000-tonners and that a two-class ship was preferable to the more traditional three-class system. Furthermore, with her capacity divided between

approximately 500 in First Class and 1,500 in Tourist, the Tourist section would have full decks from stem to stern including choice centre-ship space formerly allocated exclusively to First Class. Her overall design of 1,035 feet would make her the longest liner ever built—4 feet longer than Britain's first *Queen Elizabeth* and 7 feet longer than her illustrious predecessor, the *Normandie*.

The *France*—the third to bear that name in French Line annals—used advanced construction systems of prefabrication. After her first keel plates were put in place on October 7 1957, huge sections (some weighing as much as 50 tons) came from towns as far away as Levallois, Orleans, Paris, La Ciotat, Le Havre, Lyon, Grenoble, and Lille. Fitting them into place was something like arranging a huge jigsaw puzzle.

She was given a unique 'double bottom' that incorporated an inner keel with storage space for 3,653 tons of fuel, 117 tons of diesel oil, and 682 tons of water. In all, she could carry 8,000 tons of fuel—enough for a full return-trip Atlantic voyage without refuelling.

Madame Charles de Gaulle was godmother to the liner at the naming and launch ceremonies on May 11 1960. The General himself gave a stirring speech on the triumphs of her creation and of the special bond linking the French and American people. A day later, some 2,000 technicians, decorators, artists, and workers invaded the ship for the finishing touches. Two months later, her rudder and four propeller shafts were installed. It took three weeks to fit the monster 74-ton rudder and the 53-ton, 60-foot long shafts—the longest in the world. Aboard, some 18,000 miles of wiring (all of it colour-coded for identification) was installed, as were 1,300 telephones (1,000 for passenger use and 300 for administrative work) and 28 miles of ventilating lines fanning out from 102 air-conditioning control centres.

Model passenger staterooms were created and fitted out, right down to the last detail. They were tested and retested. For example, after sound-proofing experiments, it was found that a combination of glass fibre and marinite material worked best. The harsh overhead lighting of earlier types was discarded in favour of soft indirect lighting with a slight candle-like tint. Every detail had to be perfect.

The forward funnel, which had been built ashore, was lifted aboard in April 1961. It was of the most radical design, crowned by a pair of ailerons serving as smoke deflectors. The big wing design gave a streamlined look to the funnels themselves while lifting the smoke up and away from the ship. In addition, each stack had a rather elaborate filtering device which removed all solids from the smoke and returned them to the bowels of the ship and eventually into the sea itself.

The four massive propellers—each weighing 27 tons and measuring 18 feet in diameter—went aboard in July 1961. Sixteen months later she was ready for her trials. With only the slightest vibrations, she reached 34.13 knots, using nine-tenths of her full power (146,000 horsepower as against the potential 160,000). On January 19 she left Le Havre on a 'dress rehearsal' cruise to the Canaries—filled to capacity and proving herself beyond reproach.

Just as with many great liners before her, the *France* bedazzled the public. When she reached New York on February 8 the press were particularly struck by her modern interiors. There was a splendid array of suites on the upper decks, some large enough to include private dining rooms with special warming kitchens. There was no wood on board but creations of aluminium, formica, and plastic. The kennels on the sun deck had 20 separate quarters, each carpeted, and the walkways included a Paris milestone and a New York City fire hydrant. The theatre could seat 664 passengers on two levels and there were two swimming pools, one indoor and the other on deck covered by a glass shield. The First-Class dining room, known as the Chambord and one of the most exquisite rooms ever to put to sea, was circular with a domed ceiling and could seat 400 at a single sitting. Alongside, there was a smaller private restaurant. Unlike many other transatlantic ships, most of the *France*'s cabins—even those in Tourist Class—featured private bathroom facilities.

Interested visitors were deluged with factual literature listing such items as the 25,300 linen sheets on board, the 246,000 napkins, the 21,600 tablecloths—all of which represented 364,000 pieces weighing 94 tons! There were 47,500 pieces of silverware, 44,000 glasses, and if all of the 23,700 plates were stacked in a column they would measure

820 feet or nearly the height of New York's RCA building. Happiness, success, and amazement filled that maiden year.

The *France* settled in well on the North Atlantic route. She quickly developed a very enviable reputation. The service and decor were much praised but, in common with most earlier French Line ships, the cuisine caused many reporters and travel-writers to take to pen and paper. Craig Claiborne, an American epicure, called the *France* 'the greatest restaurant in the world'. Cosmetics queen Helena Rubinstein crossed in the liner in 1964, and at the time remarked, 'If I live to be 100, there will still be nothing better than a sea voyage.' She died a year later, aged 99! To many, the ship represented a style of crossing that was all too rapidly disappearing.

The *France* averaged 100 per cent occupancy during the summer months, the peak season for the Atlantic trade, and an amazing 70 per cent at other times. But that glitter began to tarnish in 1966, even if at a slower rate than for many other liners. The jets provided furious and persistent competition. Winter Atlantic crossings were the first to go for the *France*. Instead, she was sent to the tropics, with 1,349 in a single class, but with the handicap that she was very much the transatlantic liner. The pools were indoors or covered, and the open deck spaces were limited. The designers of the ship were far more concerned with the foggy or wet North Atlantic rather than the warm tranquillity of the Caribbean.

In 1972, the French Line decided on the ship's first world cruise, an affair that had all the attached sensationalism of a 1930s maiden voyage. Because of her size, she was too big to pass through the Panama Canal and so had to circle South America at its southern-most tip. A special tanker was despatched from the motherland for a refuelling rendezvous off Rio and giant consignments of linens and other supplies were flown ahead by air. A continuous airlift was created to and from Paris for weary crew members. And for special needs, as with one prosperous passenger, a favourite brand of champagne was flown to Hong Kong to meet the ship.

Two years later, the *France* was at its worst—the Atlantic trade had all but vanished, with the American cruise trade growing more and more competitive and fuel price increases sending the barrel rate from $35 to $95. The French government would have to extend its subsidy from $14

Some time later, a millionaire Arabian named Akram Ojjeh bought the liner from the French government for $22 million. His plan was to fill her with the Wildenstein collection of French antique furniture, which he had purchased for an additional $15 million. The scheme then went further: he would turn the ship simultaneously into a museum of French civilisation and a hotel-casino moored off Daytona Beach, Florida. Mr Ojjeh's plan subsequently amounted to nothing more than hefty dockage fees. He put the ship back on the market.

The *France* then passed into the hands of the Oslo-based Norwegian Caribbean Lines, one of the most successful companies trading on the very lucrative Miami-Caribbean circuit. The transfer cost $18 million and the ship was sent to the Hapag-Lloyd Shipyards in Bremerhaven to undergo an additional $80 million renovation and tropical orientation programme. Renamed the *Norway*, she hoisted the Norwegian colours along with those of the United Nations, as a salute to the 25 different nationalities or more represented on board. However, the key to the liner's intended operations was economy. Only one engine room would be used, creating a fuel-saving service speed of 16 knots. The staff would be reduced from its French level of 1,110 to 800, while the capacity would be increased for greatest possible revenue from 2,044 to 2,181. On board, some of the original installations were retained while others were removed and replaced with outdoor pools and lido areas, shopping arcades, discos, soda fountains, and slot machines. If the *Norway* is kept at 80 per cent capacity, she will recover her investment in seven years.

She crossed on a special Atlantic voyage in May 1980, from Oslo to New York via Southampton, and then took up her position at Miami on a weekly run to a Bahamian out-island and St Thomas. She is now the 'queen' of a very different fleet.

Gross tonnage: 66,348 (1961), 69,500 (1980)
Length overall: 1,035 feet
Width: 110 feet
Draft: 34 feet
Machinery: Steam turbines geared to quadruple screw
Speed: 30 knots (1961), 16 knots (1980)
Capacity: 501 First and 1,543 Tourist (1961); 2,181 single class (1980)
Built: Chantiers de l'Atlantique, St Nazaire, France, 1957–61

Above *On the slipways before ever reaching the waters of the Loire. Notice that the propellers have not yet been attached.*

Right *A splendid aerial photograph as the liner is eased into her berth at Manhattan's Pier 88 (Courtesy of Moran Towing).*

million to $24 million. Underwriting the Concorde seemed a much more promising venture and so, as the government's support was cut completely, the French Line had no choice but to withdraw the ship. Near the end, in September 1974, some crew members mutinied just off Le Havre, holding the ship at anchor in the Channel, demanding that she be restored and asking for 35 per cent wage increases. The attempt failed and the *France* was sent to an old pier in the backwaters of Le Havre.

France

Above *Fireboat spray welcomes the* France *on her gala arrival at New York in February* 1962.

Below *After a thorough refit, the* Norway *arrives off the Norwegian coast for the first time. Notice the huge davits on the fore deck with the unusually large tender nested between them* (Courtesy of Norwegian Caribbean Lines).

Fifty Famous Liners

Oceanic

When the *Oceanic* steamed into the Port of New York for the first time on an afternoon in April 1965, she was greeted with a mixture of responses: pride and success, curiosity, and outright suspicion and dislike. In any respect, she was unquestionably one of the most stunning liners of the 1960s.

To the Home Lines, a firm begun in 1946 with a view to transporting immigrants in second-hand ships and with links to such diverse countries as Sweden, Italy, Greece, Panama, and the United States, she represented tremendous success and advance. Not only was she the firm's first brand-new liner but one far and away larger and more luxurious than any of the previous fleet. In her design, ideas came from all of the earlier Home Lines' passenger ships and then from investigations made on numerous other liners, including the Dutch *Rotterdam*, Britain's *Canberra* and *Oriana*, Italy's *Leonardo da Vinci*, and, the biggest of all, the *France*. Something was learned from each, often modified in theory and then applied for best results. It would seem that the Home Lines asked for the very finest in overall design and performance and were given, through a brilliant combination of good planning and fortune, a vessel that startled other passenger ship-owners and that has gone forward to become one of the most successful liners ever built.

In her first 15 years, her appearance seems to have defied time. Her public spaces, save for some

reupholstering and colour changes, have worn extremely well. Her bold hull form, with practically no sheer, relatively low height, and placement of machinery aft, has been coupled with exceptionally high maintenance. Consequently, *Oceanic*'s operating results have been more than satisfactory. She managed 27.2 knots during her trial runs and has been intended to render a service speed of 25.5 knots (speed not being a requirement in the cruise trades has recently become an area for economy in the face of the rising cost of fuel oils). At the time of her maiden trip, it was said in at least one journal that the *Oceanic* would influence more subsequent passenger liners than any other ship in modern times. This has been shown to be true, at least in the sense that most other companies have sent representatives to examine the Home Lines' flagship for thoughts on their future tonnage.

At first, the *Oceanic* resembled the similar-sized *Empress of Britain* of 1931 in that she was intended for summer North-Atlantic service to the St Lawrence River ports of Quebec City and Montreal. Her European ports were to be Cuxhaven (for Hamburg), Le Havre, and Southampton, and although her original design was very much the same as it is now, she was designed to carry 400 passengers in First Class and 1,200 in Tourist. She would have revolutionised the North-Atlantic trade with her vast open-air spaces, outdoor-indoor swimming pools and private facilities in all cabins regardless of class. She was intended to cruise during the winter months—with 1,200 in a single class. New York would be her base and although the Caribbean area had the greatest lure, she could pass through Panama and had a long-distance cruising range.

Then, eight months after the *Oceanic*'s launching in Monfalcone (January 15 1963), the Home Lines reached a decision that greatly surprised the other Atlantic shipping companies. They were to abandon the service to Montreal and would use the *Homeric*, then their largest ship, on year-round cruise service between New York and Nassau in the Bahamas. The Home Lines' board were positive that aircraft represented the future of Atlantic travel and saw cruising as a lifestyle that was still in demand and which would only grow as the public at large realised the exceptional value in ship-board holiday fares. However, this strategy represented an enormous gamble. The 730-passenger, 24,000-ton *Homeric* seemed relatively safe for the 'experimental' year-round cruise service, but could the 1,200-passenger, 39,000-ton, $40 million *Oceanic* expect to earn her keep? New York in the early 1960s was still a winter-season cruise departure port and some firms, such as the Italian and Cunard Lines, even persisted in winter-time transatlantic crossings. Great attention was focussed on the new *Oceanic* in her maiden year.

The reaction was shattering. Word spread quickly in travel circles that the *Oceanic* was a magnificent ship, well designed with a wide range of facilities; for instance, every passenger cabin could be converted to a day sitting room; there was a 700-seat dining room; a 400-capacity double-level cinema; a swimming pool-cabana area, covered by a sliding glass roof called a Magrodome that could open or close within three minutes depending on the weather, which was heated by infra-red rays and had specially warmed pool waters. Her reputation was built also on two other very important ingredients: her cuisine and the performance of her staff. The choice of an Italian crew provided not only some of the best results in the restaurants but also produced a social warmth that has so endeared the ship to the American travelling public. If the *Queen Mary* earned over $600 million in her 31 years of service, the *Oceanic* will in all probability produce an equally impressive record. She paid for herself within her first five years, earned $89 million in profit over one three-year period and has averaged an enviable 92 per cent occupancy rate in her first 15 years.

The original gamble taken by Home Lines could never be regretted.

On the point of initial antipathy: the *Oceanic* first arrived amidst a labour-organised reaction to foreign-flag cruise liners. New York stevedores felt that American passenger ships would be hard hit by the effects of less-expensive foreign vessels and had their thoughts cemented when the United States Lines decided to retire the 33,000-ton *America* in the same year, a decision prompted by costly labour and her inability to compete profitably with European liners. Consequently, as the *Oceanic* sailed along the Hudson River for a fire-boat and tug reception, some banners and signs suggested 'Run-away flagship go home!' Fortunately, there was no response. Some 1,200 American travel agents sailed in the ship's inaugural trip to Nassau and returned only with the greatest of praise. The *Oceanic* quickly settled in to her favoured position.

Cunard's *Aquitania* had one of the most successful lives ever enjoyed by a major passenger liner. She gave excellent service, provided untold profits and was a continuous object of pride and joy to her owners. One can only suspect, judging by the first half of her life, that the *Oceanic* will join the ranks of such ships.

Gross tonnage: 39,241
Length overall: 782 feet
Width: 97 feet
Draft: 28 feet
Machinery: Steam turbines geared to twin screw
Speed: 26.5 knots
Capacity: Reduced to 1,200 single class (maximum of 1,602)
Built: Cantieri Riuniti dell'Adriatico Shipyard, Monfalcone, Italy, 1965

Maiden arrival of the Oceanic *in New York.*

Above *The hull of the* Oceanic *takes form in Trieste. Upper left sits the hull of the* Guglielmo Marconi *and in the background, the* Galileo Galilel.

Below *Hoisting aboard one section of the Magrodome lido deck covering, which opened as the weather dictated.*

Docking scene on the Oceanic's *maiden arrival. The stern of the* Independence *can be seen in this shot.*
(Courtesy of Moran Towing).

Fifty Famous Liners

Michelangelo

Following World War 2, the Italian Line found itself left with only four surviving passenger liners: *Conte Biancamano, Conte Grande, Saturnia,* and *Vulcania.* The remaining pre-war Italian fleet was either destroyed or lying in ruins, like the bombed and battered superships, the *Rex* and the *Conte di Savoia.* The refurbishing of the survivors was taken in hand and the slow process of building new tonnage was undertaken with the thought that great superliners were wasteful symbols of a bygone era. Future Italian liners would be more moderate in size, more economical, and much more profitable. Prior to the war, neither the *Rex* nor the *Conte di Savoia* contributed to the Italian Line's treasury.

The first new passenger ships to be built were the 27,000-ton sisters *Augustus* and *Giulio Cesare,* added in 1951–2, for the booming Italy-east coast of South America trade. Then, attention was focused on the link to New York, which was being shared between the *Saturnia* and *Vulcania* in cooperation with American Export Lines' *Constitution* and *Independence.* This was a fancier, more demanding service and so designs were developed for two rather impressive ships, filled with works of Italian art and the highest possible levels of decor. These trans-atlantic sisters were to be symbolic of Italy's merchant marine rebirth following the devastation of the war. The *Andrea Doria* came first, in January 1953, and was followed 16 months later by the *Cristoforo Colombo.* Both were received with great enthusiasm and brought promise of a new era of Italian passenger shipping.

Then, in July 1956, tragedy struck when the *Doria* was sunk off the American New England coast after colliding with the Swedish *Stockholm.* To the Italian Line, the loss of its post-war flagship was both shocking and embarrassing. A replacement was quickly ordered. This new vessel appeared in June 1960, as the country's biggest post-war liner yet, the 33,000-ton *Leonardo da Vinci.* At about the same time, the Italian directors obviously developed a new enthusiasm for superliners. They analysed the traffic requirements on the North-American service and found promising indications. The jet aircraft had not yet made its impact in the Mediterranean and therefore there were vast numbers still desirous of passenger-ship service. Furthermore, the Tourist-Class sections—far improved from their stark pre-war standard—were still used by thousands each year on the westbound voyages emigrating to America. Additional support was indicated by the six liners used by the company on the summer-season trans-atlantic run in 1960: *Leonardo da Vinci, Cristoforo Colombo, Saturnia, Vulcania, Augustus,* and *Conte Biancamano* (the latter two being specially reassigned from the South American trade). The American-Caribbean cruise trade was beginning to grow as a winter off-season service, and Italian Line wanted its share—but with highly efficient ships.

Twin superships became the order of the day and the engineering department at the firm's headquarters in Genoa was called upon to produce preliminary sketches. They would be the first major passenger liners to be built as a pair since the *Bremen*

and *Europa* of 1929. (All later ships, such as the *Queen Mary* and *Queen Elizabeth*, and even the *Rex* and *Conte di Savoia*, were in fact running-mates and not identical sisters.)

The first of these new ships was launched as the *Michelangelo*, following the post-war Italian naming policy to salute great historic figures, on September 16 1962, at the Ansaldo Shipyards in Genoa. As on all such occasions previously, a Roman Catholic Cardinal attended the ceremonies and gave the ship a formal blessing. She had her trials in April 1965, and arrived in New York for the first time on May 20. The sister ship, named *Raffaello*, was built at the Cantieri Riuniti dell'Adriatico Shipyard in Monfalcone and appeared on the Atlantic two months later, in July.

The eleven-deck *Michelangelo* was considered to be the flagship and cost a total of $45 million. She and her sister, although lighter at 45,000 tons due to the extensive use of more modern materials such as aluminium, were the longest Italian liners ever built at 902 feet overall each, exceeding the 51,000-ton *Rex*'s 879 feet.

She boasted an exceptionally unusual profile, one that is most unique to her and not easily confused with any other ship, with her huge white hull (it had been intended to use black, but white proved more attractive and more heat-resistant, particularly important in tropical cruise ports) and wide green stripe painted all around, just below the main deck. Because of the length of the hull and the colouring, the superstructure did not seem as high as it actually was. In fact, it reached five decks above the main deck. The two funnels were located further aft than they might be on any other ship and, in fact, seem to create a forward space that might have been intended for a third funnel. However, this forward section was deliberately created for the First-Class swimming pool and lido area. The 45-foot-high funnels were strongly reminiscent of the cage masts aboard early battleships and had upsweeping wind guides on the tops to keep the smoke and fumes away from the aft decks. An exhaust pipe surrounded by lattice work created both an effective and pleasing funnel design.

There were 742 passenger cabins on board which, considering the full capacity of 1,775 passengers, averaged 2.4 passengers per room. For the first time, in all three classes, on the Atlantic, every cabin had private bathroom facilities. There were 30 public

rooms including a 489-seat cinema. Arras tapestries, ceramics, and paintings were used for decoration but in sweeping modern styles. Gone were the mural-painted ceilings and columned lounges of the *Rex* and the *Conte di Savoia*. The ship had six separate swimming pools, of which three were shallow pools for children. Each of the three larger ones were infra-red heated so that passengers could sit alongside even on chilly days at sea.

The *Michelangelo* and *Raffaello* balanced the Italian Line's express service, making a return-trip voyage in approximately three weeks between Naples, Genoa, Cannes, Algeciras, and New York. Occasionally the service was extended to include Messina, Barcelona, Lisbon, and/or Casablanca. At other times, the pair went cruising, mostly to the Caribbean but periodically during their careers to Rio de Janeiro in February for the Carnival and from Genoa to the Black Sea, other Mediterranean ports, and even as far afield as Scandinavia.

During the *Michelangelo*'s first winter overhaul, which began on December 31 1965, the propellers were changed in an effort to reduce some very noticeable vibrations. During the subsequent trial runs, her best recorded speed was 31.59 knots. Much to the delight of her owners, she returned to service a more balanced liner.

However, a very serious test of her buoyancy came a few months later, on April 12, when steaming for New York she was lashed by 50-foot-high waves. Two passengers were swept into the sea and the forward portion of the superstructure was badly damaged. She arrived in New York and underwent some preliminary repairs by a dockside shipyard crew using a floating crane. She returned eventually to Genoa with her deckhouse draped in canvas covering.

Projections that the *Michelangelo* and *Raffaello* would enjoy substantial, profitable lives were incorrect. By 1970, both ships were losing money, often to the staggering ratio of $700 from the Italian government subsidy for every one of the passengers carried. On some occasions, the 775 crew members outnumbered the paying guests. There was talk of keeping the ships in service through a series of modified cost-reducing plans, one of which suggested transferring the *Raffaello* to South American service. Little was actually done and each season the ships continued to show losses, much to the government's horror but prodded on by the very powerful Italian seamen's unions. Brief strikes became common as each new rumour developed that earmarked the liners for withdrawal. Consequently, the ships were very often hard-pressed to maintain their published schedules. Even the American cruise service began to show deficits, particularly after the great fuel cost increases in 1973.

Finally, the Italian government withdrew its financial assistance and both ships were laid up. The *Michelangelo* made her last run, in June 1975, with some tearful fans on board, including the aged Duchess of Windsor. At first, the ships lay idle in Genoa and were then switched to La Spezia, anchored side-by-side and perilously close to the Mediterranean's biggest scrapyard. Newspaper reports hinted that it was not inconceivable that the ships would be scrapped on their tenth birthdays and wildly criticised the government for building them in the first place.

Several steamship lines inspected the pair but obviously found them too big for their needs. Even the Soviet Ministry of Shipping gave them a glance. In November 1975, it was reported that they would be sold to a holding company known as I G Tronado of Liechtenstein, presumably for West Germans who wanted to use the ships as floating cancer research centres. Their scheme had the liners sailing on two and three-week cruises with patients undergoing treatment, utilising a variety of cures. The project never materialised despite considerable press to the contrary. Instead, the sisters were finally sold, in February 1977, to the Shah of Iran's government for use as permanently moored military barracks. On July 8, the *Michelangelo* left Genoa for passage through the Suez Canal and final positioning at Bandar Abbas. She arrived there on the 21st, and the Iranian colours were hoisted in the presence of the Shah himself. The *Raffaello* followed some weeks later and was docked at Bushire. Each ship was rearranged to house 500 officers and 1,300 mariners from the Iranian Navy.

With the political situation undergoing such unrest in Iran, the future of the *Michelangelo* is in question. In such a remote location, she must seem very lonely.

Right *An impressive aerial view in Genoa.*

Gross tonnage: 45,911
Length overall: 902 feet
Width: 102 feet
Draft: 34 feet
Machinery: Steam turbines geared to twin screw
Speed: 26.5 knots
Capacity: 535 First, 550 Cabin and 690 Tourist; 1,200 single class for cruising
Built: Ansaldo Shipyard, Genoa, Italy, 1965

Left *The glistening modern elegance of the First-Class lounge.*

Right *Together with the* Leonardo da Vinci, *Italy's previous flagship.*

Below right *The lattice-work funnels became the identifying mark for both the* Michelangelo *and her sister the* Raffaello.

Below *The sitting area and bedroom of a First-Class suite.*

Michelangelo

Queen Elizabeth 2

In a television documentary on the great transatlantic liners seen in the United States in 1980, the *Queen Elizabeth 2*—as the last of that mighty breed—was described as 'a fugitive from modern economic realities running for her very life.' She has probably spent all her life in such a state. Poetically, she is a very modern successor to the grand heritage of the Cunard Company and, in fact, to the entire age of the ocean liner as we once knew it. Although she cruises quite often, she still makes port-to-port liner voyages but in a time when they are almost as anachronistic as travel by zeppelin. Consequently, as the final member of the Atlantic liner family, she has been the subject of enormous press (and the bulk of that aforementioned television special)—possibly more than any other liner. Ironically, most of the publicity stresses her unique 'last of an era' position and often has encouraged travellers to book a passage quickly before she (the ship) and the entire North-Atlantic passenger sea-trade are gone forever.

Realistically, while the 'Queen' and her owners have wallowed in the publicity, she has long been financially ailing, often worrisome and frequently troubled. By her tenth birthday in 1979, even when filled to the very last upper berth, she still lost untold millions for the Cunard Company and its parent owner, Trafalgar House Investments. It is a matter of great wonder how she has managed to survive into her second decade. Early on, the new management at Cunard indicated that the *Queen Elizabeth 2* was not intended as a successor to the styles and legend of the original 'Queens' and other famous Cunarders. Instead, she was a vast floating hotel, that followed the sun in between crossings on the North Atlantic. The prestige attached to, let's say, the *Queen Mary* is absent, replaced instead by a low-key reverence for a modern, moving piece of real estate. The public's regard for great liners and that of the last of the crews that serve aboard them has changed enormously from the days much covered in these pages.

The *Queen*—which was quite quickly dubbed as the *QE2*—came from the John Brown yards on the Clyde, using the same facilities that created the original *Mary* and *Elizabeth* some thirty years earlier. In the early 1960s, when Cunard was facing the reality of the *Queen Mary*'s retirement, the directors thought in terms of a 75,000-ton, three-class 'traditional' liner, that was headlined as the *Q3*. The concepts were revised when serious notice was finally taken of the enormous inroads made on the Atlantic run by the airline industry. The new ship design showed more promise: being adaptable to cruising for at least half of the year, having two classes instead of three and facilities like outdoor pools, lido decks,

big cinemas, discos, saunas, and shops that would provide a serious competitive edge over other existing liners. Surely, some members of that Cunard Board must have given thought to a more practical approach still, like building two far more economical 35,000-tonners instead. But giant concepts were persisting, not just at Cunard but with the French, who had their brand new *France*, and the Italians, who were building not one but two 45,000-ton ships. At worst, Cunard was the last company ever to think in terms of a superliner.

The order was signed, the steel ordered, and the first keel plates laid in position on June 5 1965. Cunard publicity slowly leaked enticing details about her size and innards, much in the same way as was done with the *Normandie* and the *Queen Mary*. The choice of a name held particular fascination, especially since the company had dozens of suggestions. Rumours abounded, again similar to the affairs of the *Normandie* and the *Queen Mary*. Press reports hinted that the new liner might be named *Queen Mary II, Britannia, Great Britain*, even *William Shakespeare* or *Winston Churchill*. Dramatically, the naming was left to the Queen herself, who had consented to launch the ship.

Just as the old speed-queen *Mauretania* left New York for the last time in September 1934 and the *Queen Mary* was simultaneously launched in Clydebank, the new liner was launched on September 20 1967, two days before the 31-year-old *Queen Mary* was due to sail from New York on her final transatlantic crossing. The new ship was named the *Queen Elizabeth 2.*

Her maiden voyage was scheduled for January 1969, and was in such demand that Cunard actually scheduled five separate trips that were considered to be 'maiden sailings', the longest of which was a run from Southampton, across the mid-Atlantic to the Caribbean, and then northward to New York. Her final fitting-out programme moved according to schedule, although with disturbing reports that shipyard crews were pillaging the liner's fresh interiors. Substantial amounts of materials, from door-knobs to prefabricated walls, were mysteriously disappearing. But the new 'Queen's' problems were just beginning.

She left Greenock on November 26 1968, for her first trials but encountered serious turbine troubles and other embarrassing defects. She crept back to her

builder's yard as Cunard refused to accept delivery. With repairs hopefully completed, she put into Southampton for the first time on January 2. More problems were uncovered and Cunard again refused acceptance. The maiden voyages had to be cancelled amidst widespread humiliation in the press. By the time she finally joined the company on April 18, the delays had cost £3 million on top of her $80 million total cost. The maiden voyage at long last got underway from Southampton on May 2.

Her troubles were far from over, however. By 1971, when Cunard was sold to Trafalgar, she was already losing £500,000 a year. A year later, she endured a bomb hoax in mid-Atlantic that frightened passengers and crew and demanded $350,000 in cash from the New York office. Four Royal Air Force bomb experts were dropped by parachute into the sea, quite near to the liner, and lifted aboard a scant 18 minutes before the bombs were due to go off. Another year later, in April, during a charter cruise from New York to Israel for that nation's 25th anniversary, Arab terrorists threatened to blow up the ship. So serious were the reports that crew members were given an extra £50 danger fee. Security on board was intense, military planes and ships escorted the liner in the Mediterranean, and all with the reverse effect of scaring off most potential passengers. When she docked at Ashdod, Israel, she was only half full. A year or so later, further information was made public suggesting that, during the Israeli cruise, President Gaddafi of Libya had wanted to have the vessel torpedoed by an Arab sub and it was only the intervention of President Sadat of Egypt that had prevented this.

There seemed to be no end to the difficulties. On April 1 1974, the 'Queen' was immobilised off Bermuda by boiler trouble. After two anxious days, the Norwegian cruise ship *Sea Venture* anchored nearby and heroically took off the stranded 1,630 passengers. By April 7, the 'Queen' was towed into Bermuda and given provisional repairs. In December 1975, she damaged her hull on coral reefs off Nassau and had to proceed to Newport News, Virginia with some unhappy passengers for urgent dry-docking. On July 23 1976, there was an engine-room fire in the eastern Atlantic and she was forced to reverse position and return to Southampton. Two years later, in September, she was tossed about with resulting damages in a fierce Atlantic storm.

In addition to all these problems, economic woes mounted for the *QE2.* Her annual overhauls were switched from Southampton to a dry dock in New York harbour, just miles from her regular berth, to save the costly mid-winter positioning voyage. She has had her port calls reduced enormously to cut costs, meaning an average of eight hours in New York and no overnight stays. Her owners try to keep her sailing as often as possible with revenue-producing passengers aboard. Her services ranged from a $250 two-day cruise out-to-sea to a $175,000 suite for a three-month cruise around-the-world. Fuel cost increases have seriously worried Cunard, especially since she burns off a record $80,000 per day (1980). Lastly, labour rates are staggering and continually rising, especially as the 'Queen' has remained 'all British' and not resorted to less expensive foreign staff.

Some official reports have said that the last of the Atlantic liners will continue in service, at least through the decade of the 1980s. As costs continue to rise it might be worth the British government's while to subsidise her heavily, considering her great publicity and public relations value, her unique position in history and, in reviving ocean liner ideals of the 1930s, her goodwill value.

Occasionally, during her visits to Los Angeles on world cruises, she passes in sight of the *Queen Mary.* At other times, on trips to the Caribbean, she has put into Norfolk and docked near the idle *United States.* One day, in the tropics, she might rendezvous with the former *France,* now known as the *Norway.* These are the *Queen Elizabeth 2*'s proud predecessors and together they are the last of the great age of the superliner.

Gross tonnage: 65,863 (1969), 67,107 (1977)
Length overall: 963 feet
Width: 105 feet
Draft: 32 feet
Machinery: Steam turbines geared to twin screw
Speed: 28.5 knots
Capacity: 564 First and 1,441 Tourist, 1,400 single class for cruising (1969); 604 First and 1,223 Tourist, 1,740 single class for cruising (1972); 1,820 single class for all sailings (1976)
Built: John Brown & Company Limited, Clydebank, Scotland, 1965–9

Fitting out as the last major liner to be built at the illustrious Clydebank yards.

Fifty Famous Liners

Above *The traditional excitement of the maiden arrival.*
Below *The 'Queen' in mid-Hudson, about to be swung into her berth at Pier 92.*

The great bow.

Index

1933 WORLD CRUISE of the aristocratic AUGUSTUS

Lido all the way

YOKOHAMA · PEIPING · NAGASAKI · KOBE · HILO · HONOLULU · LOS ANGELES · BALBOA · CRISTOBAL · HAVANA · NEW YORK · SHANGHAI · HONGKONG · MANILA · ZAMBOANGA · BALI · SAMARANG · BATAVIA · BANGKOK · SINGAPORE · DELI · PENANG · COLOMBO · BOMBAY · SUEZ · HAIFA · ATHENS · TRIPOLI · NAPLES · GENOA · MONTE CARLO · CANNES · GIBRALTAR · MADEIRA · NEW YORK

LUCAS TRAVEL SERVICE

ITALIAN LINE
IN COOPERATION WITH THE
AMERICAN EXPRESS COMPANY

French Line
NEW YORK
COMPAGNIE GÉNÉRALE TRANSATLANTIQUE
NEW YORK · LONDON · PARIS
FIRST CLASS—STATEROOM

HOME LINES
B

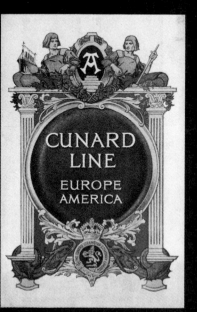

CUNARD LINE
EUROPE AMERICA

HOLLAND - JAVA

HANDBOOK FOR PASSENGERS
NEDERLAND LINE
ROYAL DUTCH MAIL
AMSTERDAM

COMPAGNIE GÉNÉRALE
TRANSATLANTIQUE